A Deed a Day

GROWING IN GRACE THROUGH KINDNESS
AND COMPASSION

Shannon Anderson

CrossLink Publishing
RAPID CITY, SD

Anderson/CrossLink Publishing
1601 Mt. Rushmore Rd, Ste 3288
Rapid City, SD 57701
www.CrossLinkPublishing.com

Ordering Information:
Quantity sales. Special discounts are available on quantity purchases by corporations, associations, and others. For details, contact the "Special Sales Department" at the address above.

A Deed a Day / Shannon Anderson. —1st ed.
ISBN 978-1-63357-323-9

Library of Congress Control Number: 2020936169

Praise for *A Deed a Day*

I can't emphasize enough how much I enjoyed this message and I firmly feel God is going to use this book to help others that have a desire to seek Him more. The layout was a fantastic mix of scripture, personal stories/testimonies, benefits, and struggles.

—**Tim Taylor,** teacher and youth pastor

*This book is dedicated to my husband, Matt,
and our girls, Emily and Maddie.*

Contents

Introduction

I was moved to tears twice in one day. It started at our back-to-school teacher meeting. Our principal spoke to us about the procedures we needed to review the first week of school.

We were used to practicing all kinds of things in our classrooms—how and where to line up for lunch and recess, what to do for arrival and dismissal, and where to go for fire and tornado drills.

These seemed like pretty ordinary reminders. But then he sat down, paused, and looked down before speaking. "I purposely saved this last part for the end of our meeting. We need to go over some *new* safety precautions."

When his normally upbeat, disc jockey voice turned somber, we knew where this was heading. Active shooter drills. For the last two years, we had practiced these drills. We simply called them lockdown drills. We used to be very vague with the kids about what we were doing.

When the announcement was made over the speaker system, we had to hurry over, lock the classroom door, close the blinds, and usher our students to a corner away from windows. Students sat silently in the dark until the principal came back on the announcements to tell us the drill was over. The kids weren't *too* phased by this because we didn't make a big deal out of it. Discussion was kept to a minimum in an attempt to not tip the kids off to the real reasons we were doing this kind of drill.

I remember making up stories like, "If someone stole something from a house, then ran away from the police, he might come into the school to hide from them. We'd need to be safe in our classrooms where he couldn't come in and hide. We also wouldn't want to be in the way if the police came in to find him." I made sure they didn't think about a lockdown as being some kind of danger to them, but rather it was to be out of the way if something like *that* happened.

With the rise in school shootings over the past couple of years, it became important to take this to a new level. We had to be more transparent about our safety precautions. Many kids were seeing or hearing about the school shootings on the news or social media, so we needed to assure them that they were safe at our school.

Our drills started to look a lot different. We had to tell the kids they had permission to dart out of the building and run away. A building tour, sharing all of the exits, was required. We had to find ways to talk to kids about "bad" people who may come in and try to hurt someone. The look of fear and shock filled their sweet faces. I'll never forget it.

Here we were, taking this yet a step further. Our principals had attended a training and learned more about the urgency of our need to do more. This meant locked classroom doors at *all* times, evacuation routes, teaching kids to throw things at a person threatening them, and directions to *not* let a student back in the room after the door is securely locked during a lockdown. It was just too much to hear.

We also had to change our morning routine. Normally the kids would gather in the gym in designated areas by class upon arrival. They hung out, played games on their iPads, or read until it was time to go down to the classrooms. This had to change since that meant we had our entire student body in one open place. If an active shooter came in, it would be too difficult to move hundreds of kids through a few narrow exits in a short amount of time. This thought gave me chills.

Even our smallest kids, the preschoolers, had to now learn to fight back, run hard, hide, or lock themselves in someplace. How were we supposed to have this conversation? How do you create a safe, risk-free environment of positivity in your classrooms with this cloud hanging over your heads? I was overcome with visions of their little faces, so happy to come to school and learn the alphabet. So eager to make friends and use their new Paw Patrol lunchboxes.

I tried to ease my mind, thinking, *in the rare event this did happen in our town, no one would target our little kids.* It was much more likely to happen in the middle or high school. That less-than-comforting thought immediately snapped to thoughts of my daughter, who would be a freshman in our high school.

How can there be so much evil in the world? How could anyone want to harm students and teachers? How did we get to this point? When and why did this wickedness become so prevalent?

I prayed. "Father, please protect our school and all schools from angry people who want to harm our kids. Help our kids to know that this isn't how all people are. Help them to seek kindness and to grow up to help others and not hurt them. Stir the hearts of those who are angry to seek you and not seek revenge or commit heinous crimes."

I spent the rest of the day preparing my classroom for the kids who would be my world during that school year. I intentionally scheduled time at the end of each day for character-building activities. We would participate in friendship projects, service projects, and many other activities to teach students to build up others and use their words and deeds for good. This would need to be planned in and prioritized.

After finally calling it a day, I drove home. I decided to sit on the sunny front porch in the fresh air to sift through the mail, read the paper, and relax a bit before preparing dinner.

People in my community addressed many letters to me. I smiled, remembering that several kindhearted people had responded to my Facebook request to sponsor a child in my room for nine dollars. This would assure the child would receive at least the dollar book in the book order each month for the nine months of the school year.

Sure enough, I opened several envelopes with checks for nine dollars to help out kids who normally wouldn't be able to afford the monthly books. What a blessing. Then I opened one for twenty dollars. I was so touched that this check would help *two* kids get books for the year. Someone who gave nine dollars was a blessing, but to go above and beyond what was asked was truly heartwarming. I wasn't prepared for the last envelope though.

I recognized the name on the return address as a cashier who worked at a local store. She was one of the friendliest people you'd meet. Once she learned your name, she'd warmly greet you and chat with you as you entered the store. I opened the envelope and pulled out a letter. She simply said, "I recently got a bonus at work and couldn't be happier than to share it with your class. Can we keep this private? P.S. I love to read."

Inside was a check for one hundred dollars. My eyes filled up. *There is good in this world. There is kindness, and there is hope.*

I share my emotional day with you as a reminder that now, more than ever, there's a need to spread kindness and hope. My prayer is that your family can experience the blessings our family experienced by striving to think of others more and ourselves less. It truly is a shift in mindset and having a heart for doing what is pleasing to the Lord.

As you read, though, I think you'll see how this book isn't just about doing one deed a day. At least I sure hope it isn't. My heart for this book is to show you how our family, a group of Christians, trying to figure life out, took a step of faith to grow our faith. We felt convicted of our selfishness and sought out ways to love others. In this process, we learned to love God more. The overflow of God's love caused us to want to make our lives matter by making a difference in the lives of others.

Colossians 1:10 says, "Then the way you live will always honor and please the Lord, and your lives will produce every kind of good fruit. All the while, you will grow as you learn to know God better and better." And *that's* what it's all about.

CHAPTER 1

The Breaking Point

Philippians 2:3-4: "Don't be selfish; don't try to impress others. Be humble, thinking of others as better than yourselves. Don't look out only for your own interests, but take an interest in others, too."

I cast a warning glare and mouthed the words, "Just a minute!" as my daughter tugged my hand. I was stirring chili with the other hand and balancing the phone between my shoulder and chin. The clothes dryer buzzer sounded as my husband walked in with our other daughter.

Maddie sniffed the air with a look of disgust and asked if *that smell* was our dinner. The dog was scratching at the door, and we had about twenty minutes to eat before we had to take the girls to youth group. My husband seemed a bit annoyed that dinner was not already on the table. The girls started arguing about who had to let the poor dog back into the house.

Among the sounds of scratching, bickering, and the clanging of dishes, the TV was advertising the new toys and gadgets available as we approached the holidays. I reached for the remote and pressed the mute button as we sat down to eat. The girls commented on the commercials, forgetting all they already had to be thankful for. I cringed when they blurted their requests.

"I want that!" said Maddie.

"Can you get me that?" Emily asked.

"Do you think Grandma will buy that for us?" begged Maddie.

"How about we say grace and give thanks for this food and for what we already have before we get carried away with what we *think* we need?" I sternly warned.

Bowing our heads, I prayed, "Lord, thank you so much for all of our many blessings. Help us to remember how blessed we are and to not take that for granted. I pray that as the Christmas season approaches, we will remember that it is all about you, Lord, and not about us. Please guide us to be more like you. We love you, Lord. Amen."

That night, as I pulled back my covers, I had a heavy heart thinking about how selfish we had become and how mindless our family's routines were. We were taskmasters who performed each day's activities as if we were on an assembly line. Absorbed in our own lives, it seemed like our consideration toward those around us dwindled on a daily basis. I cried into my pillow, at my breaking point. I didn't want to keep living just for *our* needs. I didn't want to keep being steered by what the *next* thing to do was. I wanted to be steered by what the *right* thing to do was.

It took getting to a breaking point to cause me to seek the Lord more and pray for discernment. Bishop TD Jakes said that a seed can't grow and become the tree it is within without breaking. Maybe I needed to break to allow God to get through to me. Sticking with this metaphor, I realized that to grow strong in our faith, we were going to need to get rooted in God and get our nourishment from the Son.

Thankfully, God *is* love and can teach us through *tough* love (1 John 4:8; Proverbs 3:12). He allowed us to get to the point that we were being so unkind and uncaring that it was uncomfortable. Author Deidra Riggs said that it is "[t]hrough our brokenness—despite our brokenness—that God transforms us." Further, "Nothing is beyond God's capacity, ability, or desire to redeem, restore and reconcile." (*One*, 2017, p. 133)

We needed to do something to bring back some meaning into our lives. It needed to be something that would refocus our own agendas and energize us toward God's plan that we each have.

I wondered how we had gotten off track. *Didn't we used to be more thoughtful? The girls grew up seeing us help each other around the house. Had we spoiled them? Did we need to have them do more chores? Did we need to give them less on birthdays and holidays?*

Maybe we needed to work on our faith journey with the kids. After all, *we* were definitely a work in progress. With Matt's work schedule, we didn't always get to go to church as a family consistently. (He worked nights and every other weekend.)

We did make sure the kids participated in youth group each week though. We prayed together but didn't really participate in any Bible studies or read the Bible regularly. I tried to look for guidance in a book my friend recommended, the *Bible Promise Book*.

I dug out my *Bible Promise Book* from my nightstand and scanned the table of contents. Selfishness? Greed? Ungratefulness? None of those were listed, so I grabbed my Bible from the top drawer. I searched the concordance in the back for what I could study up and share with Emily and Maddie on generosity, serving others, and being unselfish.

Then this verse hit me right between the eyes. 1 Timothy 5:10: "She must be well respected by everyone because of the good she has done. Has she brought up her children well? Has she been kind to strangers and served other believers humbly? Has she helped those who are in trouble? Has she always been ready to do good?"

Wow. Guilty as charged. Not only was I not doing a good job of raising my girls to love and serve others unselfishly, but I was not being a good role model for this either. Then there was Acts 20:35, when Paul spoke to the members of a church, "And I have been a constant example of how you can help those in need by working hard. You should remember the words of the Lord Jesus: 'It is more blessed to give than to receive.'"

Oh, I worked hard; that couldn't be argued. But was I working hard to further God's kingdom and to help others, or was I working hard to better myself and my career? Reality check.

Grabbing a pen and legal pad, I started jotting down verses. I knew I needed to be in the Word more and get rid of the big plank in my eye before pointing out the specks in the eyes of my family (Matthew 7:3). I made a conscious commitment to find a way to steer all of us in a new and better direction.

Plunging back in his Word, I found 1 Timothy 6:18–19 helpful: "Tell them to use their money to do good. They should be rich in good works and generous to those in need, always being ready to share with others. By doing this they will be storing up their treasure as a good foundation for the future so that they may experience true life." Wasn't that the goal? To experience true life for Christ?

Of course, being ages six and nine at the time, the girls didn't have much money to use for good works, but that wasn't really the point. Serving others in some way is even more generous than using money in little kid "currency." But if they wouldn't even budge on walking over to let the dog back in the house, how could I convert them to becoming cheerful givers and servers?

I had an idea. Oprah's gratitude journal. If a gratitude journal helps people to focus on all they have, instead of their have-nots, what if we started a journal or diary of some kind? I loved the idea of being thankful for what we had, but it still focused us on ourselves. The Lord calls us to be grateful and thankful for our many blessings. He also calls us to serve and be more like him.

What if the focus of *our* diary was on how we serve others? We could do some kind of kind act or good deed for others and record and reflect on that.

Prayer

> Lord, thank you for the many blessings you provide us every day. We especially thank you for sending your Son as a gift of salvation. Help us to grow in our faith and our desire to be more like you. Show us ways we can serve and be a vessel of your love, kindness, and mercy. Amen.

Reflection

1. In what ways do you see your family focusing on self?

2. How would it change your relationships in the home if you focused on each other more?

3. Read 1 John 3:18: "Dear children, let's not merely say that we love each other; let us show the truth by our actions." Why is this verse so important to remember and do?

4. What other examples in the Bible can you find where people have done selfless acts to help or serve someone? What was the outcome?

CHAPTER 2

The Family Meeting

Hebrews 10:24: "Let us think of ways to motivate one another to acts of love and good works."

The ideas for growing our faith and promoting good will toward others started to take shape after digging in the Bible for guidance. When you specifically look for and pray about an issue, if it is God's will for you, you can trust that his hand will be at work.

I don't believe in luck or coincidence. The verses I found were definitely in front of me for a reason. Most of the verses I came across seemed to be sharing the same message as James 2:18: "Now some may argue, 'Some people have faith; others have good deeds.' But I say, 'How can you show me your faith if you don't have good deeds? I will show you my faith *by* my good deeds'" (italics mine). Hebrews 13:16 also spoke to me: "And don't forget to do good and to share with those in need. These are the sacrifices that please God."

Maybe the best way to strengthen our faith and shape how we think is through consciously making an effort to do something for others on a regular basis. But how? It's easy to say, "We need to think of others more. Let's try to do more favors and help out." Even if that worked, it would be temporary, at best. There had to be an accountability measure. We needed to somehow check in with each other and show this was important.

I drove a few blocks to a CVS store and purchased a basic black-and-white composition journal. Instead of a gratitude journal, we would create a diary of our good deeds. Once home, I got out a black permanent marker and labeled it "Our Deed Diary" and asked Matt and the girls to come into the living room.

They came in and plopped on the couch. I sat on the floor in front of them, holding the journal. "We need to have a family meeting," I said. They all looked at me like I had lost my mind.

I told my husband and our daughters, "I want us all to think about doing a kindness for others every day. It could be for each other or for people outside our home. We want to focus less on ourselves and brighten someone else's day in the process."

Maddie asked, "What's a good deed?"

"A good deed is doing something nice for someone else that the person wasn't expecting. It could be as simple as making a card for your teacher or going out of your way to give someone a compliment for something. You could help your sister with her chores or make your bed without being asked. We're just trying to think of things that would make another person smile," I answered.

"We're going to record our deeds every day and discuss them at dinner," I explained. The girls seemed excited at the prospect of this new "game" we were playing. My husband rolled his eyes. I said a little prayer, "Lord, please bless this experience as we bless others. Please help us all to be more like you and serve others joyfully. Forgive our selfishness and provide us wisdom to know how to best be a light and spread kindness."

When I first conceived of this project, I thought that one deed a day was too easy. Let me tell you; it's harder than it seems. We all, of course, do things for others on a regular basis, but this had to be something above and beyond what we already normally did. Sending birthday cards to people that we already send cards to every year would not count. This had to be an unexpected effort on our part.

Sometimes when we read in the Bible about doing good deeds, we see verses like Romans 12:13: "When God's people are in need, be ready to help them. Always be eager to practice hospitality." Or Psalm 112:9: "They share freely and give generously to those in need. Their good deeds will be remembered forever." These verses speak specifically to helping those in need.

Helping those in need is obviously a great way to be selfless and make a difference in the lives of others. That was certainly something we could strive for. However, I felt like we were so far to the other end of *self*-focused that we needed to not just limit our acts to helping the needy. We needed to reach out in general kindness to anyone. My motive was to create mindsets of purpose and intention. We needed to be seeking out opportunities to bless others even in small ways daily. If we did this, life-changing habits could be formed and become a part of our internal drive.

I opened our Deed Diary and wrote the date: November 2, 2009. Then I wrote each of our names in a list underneath. Holding it open, I showed my family where we would write the next day's deeds. We brainstormed a few ideas.

Especially for the girls, we tried to focus on how they could show they care by taking initiative in helping instead of waiting to be asked. It is more meaningful to serve when you are seeking to serve, not just complying with what you *have* to do.

"Remember, it means a lot more to someone when you are thoughtful and see a need and help out. I can't tell you how thrilled I would be if you put your clothes in the hamper without being asked or let the dog in or out just because you knew it needed to be done. It's also a big deal if you do something with a cheerful heart. When you are asked to do a favor or help, you could do it without grumbling or complaining. That would count as doing something for our Deed Diary. It doesn't have to be a huge, planned thing."

I got up and grabbed my Bible and returned to the floor in front of them. Opening to 2 Corinthians 9:7, I shared this verse, "You must each decide in your heart how much to give. And don't give reluctantly or in response to pressure. For God loves a person who gives cheerfully."

"God gives us so much and does so much for us. We need to give and do for others too," I said. Both girls seemed to understand. The true test would be if they followed through the next day.

Prayer

> Lord, we pray that you will give us wisdom to know what needs to be done and that you would give us the desire in our hearts to do for others cheerfully. Please help us to be selfless and serve others without complaining. Help us show our faith through the kindness we spread.

Reflection

1. Why do you think it is so important to record your intentional acts of kindness?

2. Why is it important for everyone in the family to participate?

3. It doesn't seem like doing one good deed a day would be difficult. Why do you suppose it is for so many people?

4. Read Titus 2:14: "He gave His life to free us from every kind of sin, to cleanse us, and to make us His very own people, totally committed to doing good deeds." How does doing a good deed each day work toward this in at least a small way?

CHAPTER 3

The First Dozen Days

First Peter 3:11: "Turn away from evil and do good. Search for peace, and work to maintain it."

As we got ready for school that week, I reminded everyone of our Deed Diary. "Don't forget to do something nice for someone! We'll write it all down tonight." I couldn't wait to hear each story.

Maddie spoke up, "Do you want some cereal, Mom?"

I smiled. "Sure, Maddie! I'll take some Cheerios with a banana sliced up on top. That was really nice of you."

The neighbor called before I finished my last bite. Matt answered. "Can you give our girls a ride to school today?"

Matt smiled. "Yep, I'll be right over." He put his phone back in his pocket. "Looks like I get to take care of my deed right off the bat too."

We all headed off for the day in high spirits. After school, I dropped Emily off at dance practice and brought Maddie home. I started dinner, then sat down to write in a card for a runner friend of mine going through a hard time.

Maddie came out of her room with a pair of jeans in her hand. "Mom, I wore out the knees in these pants. Should I throw them out?"

"You could run them across the street to our neighbor. She always makes denim quilts for others for Christmas and could probably use them."

Before long, Matt came home with Emily, and we finally sat down to eat. We prayed for our food, and I pulled out the Deed Diary. "OK, guys. Here we go! "Matt, what did you do for someone today?"

"I gave the neighbor girls a ride to school, remember?" He seemed very proud.

"That's right, yes. OK, Emmy, what did you do?"

"I got out the mats for the dance teacher without being asked. I'll let Lucy out right now too."

"Nice! OK, Maddie, what did you do today?"

"I got you breakfast and gave my jeans to Heather to use for her quilts."

"Awesome! Well, I made a card for a friend going through a tough time, to encourage her."

I wrote down all of these acts of kindness and put the notebook in a drawer. We talked a little about how it felt to help others, and we chatted about some ideas for tomorrow. I drifted off to sleep that night with high hopes.

The rest of that week and part of the following week were filled with many thoughtful acts and favors. From helping out teachers, to noticing chores around the house that needed done, to donating our time to serve others. The "deed a day" was off to a great start. Or so we thought.

The dozenth day dinner was disappointing. When we sat down to eat, not one of us had something to share about a kindness that day. We cleaned up the table, and Emily and I headed to family fun night at school.

We helped out in the room with the cake walk. It was kind of like musical chairs, except when the music stops, you want to be the last one standing because you win a cake! I let Emily participate a few times, and she ended up winning a white cake with sprinkles. She was as happy as a clam to be able to surprise Maddie and Matt with the delicious cake. "Dad and Maddie will be so excited!" she said.

A first-grade boy and his parents joined the game for the ninth or tenth time. The mom explained to the boy, "Honey, even if you don't win this time, we need to go ahead to the other rooms and do those activities. There's a craft room and a cookie decorating room too!"

The song ended, and a fifth-grade girl won the German chocolate cake that round. The boy teared up as his dad motioned for them to leave the room. Emily tugged on my shirt. "Mom, can I give that boy my cake?"

I beamed. "Of course! That is so sweet of you!"

Emily grabbed the cake from the counter and walked it over to the boy. "Here. You can have my cake," she said.

The boy looked at his parents hopefully. They thanked Emily and walked out, holding the cake, appreciative of her gesture.

"I'm so proud of you, Emmy! That was very thoughtful, and you made that little boy's night. Do you want to play again and try to win another cake?"

"Is it OK if I go to one of the other rooms to play a game?" Emily asked.

"Sure! I'll come and join you when I finish my shift," I said.

I found Emily in the Bingo for Books room. There were books spread out on tables, as well as small toys and stuffed animals. Emily held up a little poodle she had won. "Awww, that's cute," I said. "Are you ready to decorate a cookie and head home?"

"Yep. Since I don't have a cake to surprise Dad and Maddie with, I'm going to give Maddie this dog and decorate an extra cookie for Dad."

We left feeling good about family night. It was fun to help out, to see families enjoying time together, and to spread a few smiles in the process. I had a renewed hope that the seeds being planted would continue germinating in the girls' hearts. The dozenth day wasn't a dud after all.

Prayer

> Lord, thank you for your many blessings. I pray that you will continue to stir our hearts to seek ways to show Christ's love through kind actions. Please help us all to find ways to demonstrate your goodness through selfless acts. Forgive us for the times we fail to shine for you when opportunities arise. Help us to recognize and seek out these opportunities—not to check off a good deed for the day but to glorify you.

Reflection

1. Why is it good to seek out ways to be kind outside of your home environment?

2. What are your thoughts on the research that states that it takes a minimum of twenty-one days to form a new habit? Do you think it takes longer to form the habit of doing a deed a day?

3. Read 3 John 1:4 together: "I could have no greater joy than to hear that my children are following the truth." Why is it such a joy to see your children serve others? Why is it so important for our children to see *us* serve others unselfishly?

4. Share a time that you did something for another person. Think about your motivation. Was it out of love, out of obligation, to fulfill a need the person had, because you felt moved to do so, or some other reason?

CHAPTER 4

Christ's Hands and Feet

James 2:18: "Now someone may argue, Some people have faith: others have good deeds. But I say, How can you show me your faith if you don't have good deeds? I will show you my faith *by* my good deeds" (italics mine).

The road was a bit rocky for the next couple of weeks, with someone forgetting to intentionally plan something or just not doing a special kindness here and there. Looking over our first month, some of the acts we recorded were a bit of a stretch. For example, one night, Maddie's kindness was that she didn't tattle on anyone all day. One of Emily's was throwing away a wrapper. I'll admit, one of mine was that I "let" the girls have friends over on a night when I was exhausted.

So, even though I'm not proud of some of these more meager deeds, we were still making it a point to reflect each night on our progress or shortcomings. We were also more mindful of opportunities as they presented themselves. I think we really caught our groove though when we started to reflect on the reason we should be trying to serve others in the first place.

I remember seeing a Youtube video one day, called "The Good-O-Meter." (Central films, 2007) It showed people at heaven's gate handing over their life files and stepping on a scale.

Even those with many good works were rated "not good enough" to enter if they didn't believe in Christ's salvation.

One person, with a thick file of sinful acts, looked condemned, until Christ stepped on the scale for him. This, of course, resulted in the scale saying "good enough!" The skit dramatized the fact that we are all sinners but have the saving grace of our Lord if we only believe that he sacrificed his life to forgive us.

I showed this video to our girls. I asked them, "If you can still get into heaven without good deeds, why do you think we should do them?"

Emily said, "To be nice to people?"

Maddie said, "To be good?"

"Yes, we should be nice and good to people, but there's a more important reason we should show kindness to others. We want everyone to know about Christ's love for us by being his hands and feet. Our hearts should be so full of gratitude and love for Jesus that it overflows into how you treat others. When others see this, they will want to know why you are different. They will want to experience the joy we have in loving others."

We are called to imitate Christ's standard of love. He is the one we should try to be like. Think about if everyone strived to be like Christ, what a peaceful existence we would enjoy. If you've ever been to a Christian camp or retreat, it feels like a little taste of heaven. You are surrounded by other believers. There are people there serving you, and you feel joy in helping others. There are times of worship and praise. The goal is to grow closer to God, grow your faith, and learn more about his Word while you are there.

In these situations, we are in harmony because we are all tied to one mission and united by our belief in the one true God. Think about an orchestra or choir. They tune their instruments or find the beginning note by listening to one note. If they were to tune to each other, then together, they would not sound good. They have to tune to that one "perfect" note to be in tune together. If we can all get tuned in to Christ's perfect love and try our best to show that to others, we can be in harmony with others too.

There is a beautiful song called "They Will Know We Are Christians by Our Love." If you listen to the lyrics, it unfolds some of the important truths of how we can show this:

"We can walk hand in hand//we can work side by side//we can guard each other's dignity and save each other's pride." By uniting as believers and working together, we can uplift others and help those in need.

The girls seemed to understand the deeper meaning behind our composition notebook. With a new mindset in place, our dinner conversations took new turns. As Christmas approached, we were naturally doing more things for others, out of a love-filled spirit.

Some of our acts included more meaningful things, such as inviting elderly friends to events with us, creating a play or songs for relatives to enjoy, saying thank-you on a regular basis to those who serve food and clean at school, making sacrifices for others, and giving more than receiving.

As Christmas grew nearer, some wonderful changes were happening. We were all demonstrating Christ's love in bigger ways. Matt took care of me when I was sick; I started playing the keyboard for our church praise band; Emily started donating clothing and toys; Maddie found ways to help around the house. These were things that normally would have taken a little prodding.

Our Christmas was more about thoughtfulness than gifts. Matt spent time snowblowing the neighbor's driveway. I let the girls use all of the gift cards I received to purchase needed dance items and clothes. The girls got along better. What normally may have been a scuffle over who got to choose the game they would play became a more agreeable conversation. We cooked food and baked for other families. These simple things warmed our hearts.

Although these gestures were small, God showed *his* ultimate love through a *small* package too. Think about it. He sent Jesus as a little baby on Christmas. He could have sent Jesus as a grown man, but he chose to bring him into the world as a small bundle of joy. Those around him got to see how something small could become life-changing when shared with others.

As Christmas break was drawing to a close, we made New Year's goals that were far more significant than in the past. Matt's goal was to be more patient with others. Emily's goal was to control her temper with her sister. Maddie wanted to try to pray every night before bedtime. My goal was to read the entire Bible in one year.

In the past, we had goals like, eating less junk food, watching less TV, and other less life-altering aspirations. When we first started the Deed Diary over a month before, it seemed like more of a temporary experiment to "fix" a selfish season of time. Now it seemed natural to seek out ways to help or share. Each day brought more opportunities to shine Christ's love through our everyday lives. I was so thankful to see God working through our family.

Prayer

> Lord, thank you for your provision. We are so thankful to have enough to give to others. You are the great provider. We know that we are not able to come close to doing as much as you do for us, but we strive to show your love through our daily lives. Thank you for teaching us your caring ways and for the gift of your Holy Spirit.

Reflection

1. Discuss how the good deeds we do show Christ's love, but Christ's love is what causes us to do good.

2. Watch the YouTube video, "The Good-O-Meter." What are your reactions to this portrayal of God's judgement of what is good enough?

3. Does your family set New Year's resolutions or goals? What are the benefits you reap from the goals you set? What benefits do others reap from your goals?

4. Read Matthew 5:14–16: "You are the light of the world— like a city on a hilltop that cannot be hidden. No one lights a lamp and then puts it under a basket. Instead, a lamp is placed on a stand, where it gives light to everyone in the house. In the same way, let your good deeds shine out for all to see, so that everyone will praise your heavenly Father." Discuss how doing good for others is not to just be good or nice but to shine Christ's light in you for others to see.

CHAPTER 5

Focus

B ut Martha was distracted by the big dinner she was preparing. She came to Jesus and said, "Lord, doesn't it seem unfair to you that my sister just sits here while I do all the work? Tell her to come and help me." But the Lord said to her, "My dear Martha, you are worried and upset over all these details! There is only one thing worth being concerned about. Mary has discovered it, and it will not be taken away from her." (Luke 10:40–41)

The story of Martha and Mary is often told in reference to being too busy to understand what is really important in life. Although hard work is praised in the Bible, focusing too much on the to-do list and not enough on the right motivations can be a form of idolatry.

In our household, we operate on the school calendar. Our school year is quite busy, but we do tend to get into a routine that allows for a daily schedule. Once we started adding a deed a day as part of our daily routine, we got into a routine and maintained it. Each night, our dinner conversation was about our experiences as we shared kindness.

The rest of the school year allowed us many more opportunities to seek God's will and feel his presence. We were keeping our New Year's goals, keeping up with our Deed Diary, and growing in our journey of faith. The girls attended youth group on Wednesday nights, and we attended Sunday services regularly.

As we approached summer, I didn't think our "streak" would be in danger. But then you blink, and before you know it, you are even busier than during the school year. How is that possible? As a teacher, you'd think having the summer off would mean there was less to do. That's not the case.

Now instead of just cooking dinner, you are also making lunches, which means double the shopping, preparing, and cleanup normally required. Then there are the summer sports, camps, and activities to drive the kids to and watch—you have to go on vacation and to the swimming pool! Can't forget to plant a garden and visit all of the people you promised you would see when summer arrives!

The summer is a welcome break from the normal routine and not quite long enough to establish a steady rhythm or new routine. It seems like we hit the ground running, and before we know it, school starts up again. I love the chance to be a stay-at-home mom in the summer. I love preparing healthy meals for my family and taking time to catch up on cleaning, organizing, scrapbooking, and other tasks that don't make the cut during the school season.

The girls love having the chance to sleep in, hang out, swim, and have fun with friends. Summer is the time we have more sleepovers, take fun trips, and learn new things. I spend a great deal of time in my classroom, preparing for the next year. We have our annual garage sale, visit family, and go to parks. There just seems to be more to do and more daylight to do it in.

If you haven't figured it out by now, with the title of this chapter and the reference to Martha and Mary, I'll spill the beans. We lost our focus over the summer. Big time.

I couldn't in good conscience write this book about doing a good deed a day for a year without being totally honest with you.

We didn't record a single thing in our Deed Diary over the summer that first year.

It isn't that we didn't think of others. We didn't stop doing kind things. We simply didn't take the time to write them all down. Thankfully, we had developed a mindset about the importance of helping and serving. We also understood the reason we should be kind to others—as an extension of Christ's love. Those are the two most important things that came from the Deed Diary.

Still, since we weren't writing down our deeds or discussing them as often, they started to take a back seat to our summer busyness. As important as Martha thought it was to prepare dinner and worry about the details, the truth is, she was concerned about the wrong things. It's easy to get wrapped up in all of the summer activities and try to cram them all in but forget about some of the most important things.

I could have left this part out, but I want you to know that we are human and we fell short. We were not diligent in keeping up with our accountability measure and are thankful for God's grace. He is so merciful when we miss church, patient when we get behind in our Bible studies, and forgiving when we are selfish.

Thankfully, the start of the school year always gets us settled into necessary routines. There is so much to fit in and figure out with school hours, dance classes, children's choir, church, youth group, girl scouts, work schedules, and various other events and adventures. They are all good things, but they require planning. As August came back around, this was a good time to reestablish our intentional acts of kindness on a daily basis. I missed our thoughtful conversations at dinner when we shared how we served others. We kicked off the school year with a renewed commitment. Here is our August 22, 2010, entry:

Madison: Donated a bookbag to a child without one.
Emily: Helped Madison open a container and gave me a shoulder rub.

Me: Donated items for a kindergarten classroom.
Matt: Ran to the store to get milk before dinner.

Each of these may seem like trivial acts, but what if you were
that kid who had to start school without a bookbag and got
one from someone who noticed? What if you were struggling
with something and got the exact assistance you needed? What
if someone reached out with a loving touch to ease your tense
muscles? What if your classroom needed supplies and someone
happily donated them to you? What if you did all you could to get
dinner on the table in time, only to realize you were out of milk,
and someone went and got it for you?

Not only did these gestures meet practical needs, but they
also made the recipients feel cared for and important. The more
you help others feel loved, the more thankful you are for God's
provision in allowing you to bless and serve others. Jesus tells
us in Matthew 10:8 that we should give as freely as we have received. We can refocus ourselves by thinking about how much
we have been given and show this gratitude by giving to and
serving others.

Once we refocused our intentions and purpose, we were back
on track again. The girls both donated to the food pantry, we
helped people with rides, and visited those going through sick-
ness and surgeries. One of my favorite acts was simply buying
some cookies. We went to the bakery and picked up a dozen
iced sugar cookies. (They had rainbow icing and smiley faces on
them.) We asked the cashier to bag them up individually. I gave
the girls each five bags to hand out to people throughout the day.
I kept a couple to give out too. When we were about to cross the
street to our school that morning, Maddie asked, "Can you stop
the van? I want to give the crossing guard one of my cookies!"

Maddie started to really pay attention to others. She started
sharing things like, "I noticed some kids on recess with no one
to play with, so I asked them to play." She saw when kids didn't

have things like gloves and hats. Maddie was intentionally trying to help people. Not because she could write it down but because she was becoming more compassionate for others.

Acts of kindness that may seem trivial actually could mean the world to a person who is hurting or losing hope. Whether you make a trip to a hospital to visit someone hours away or pick a flower on the way to a friend's house, as Aesop said, "[n]o act of kindness, no matter how small, is ever wasted." We should never get tired of doing what is good (Galatians 6:10).

If we can fully focus on others instead of ourselves, we are being more like Jesus. Martha was so worried about getting dinner ready and having everything perfect that she forgot where her focus should be. We got so busy and caught up in our summer schedules, we forgot our focus as well. Instead of giving up the idea or thinking, "Well, we blew it!" we got ourselves back on track and recommitted our calling as Christians. God is so good and patient with us.

Prayer

> Lord, we are thankful for our many blessings, which include your mercy, patience, and forgiveness. We want to shine a light for you and serve others. Please give us the focus and wisdom to know who is in need and the opportunities to be your hands and feet. We want to be kind to others, as you have been kind to us. I pray that people may see Christ's love as our motivation and that they would want to learn more about you to experience the joy only your hope brings.

Reflection

1. Have you ever committed to something on your journey of faith and slipped? It could be to join a Bible study group, to read a certain number of pages in the Bible each week, or to attend church every Sunday. What caused you to slip? What did you do when you realized you weren't following through?

2. What kinds of accountability steps can we take to stay focused on our goals? What can we do to help us remember the right things to focus on?

3. Read Psalm 65:3–5: "Though we are overwhelmed by our sins, you forgive them all. What joy for those you choose to bring near, those who live in your holy courts. What festivities await us inside your holy Temple. You faithfully answer our prayers with awesome deeds, O God our savior. You are the hope of everyone on earth, even those who sail on distant seas." How does God answer our prayers with awesome deeds?

CHAPTER 6

Secondhand Blessings

First Peter 4:10: "God has given each of you a gift from his great variety of spiritual gifts. Use them well to serve one another."

When you think of something being secondhand, you may think of a consignment store, a garage sale, or having to wear your sister's hand-me-downs. Or worse, you may think of something like secondhand smoke. In any case, you probably aren't super excited about whatever is being offered or passed around. It may be defective, worn out, or even cause cancer!

Secondhand blessings are different. Special even. We can all agree that all of the blessings we *receive* are from God (Ephesians 1:3). Think about this though. All of the blessings we are able to *give* to others are from God too. When we do something for someone else, it is through God's power that we are able to serve. When we buy something for someone, we are only able to acquire the money to buy the items through God's provision of a job and the ability to do that job.

You see, all blessings are secondhand when they come from us because they originate from God. This is when secondhand is a very good thing. There is nothing defective, worn out, or cancer-causing about God's blessings that he delivers through us. God gives us many gifts because he wants us to use them to show his love. You are his vessel. Many times, you are a scheduled blessing for someone—a secondhand blessing.

Have you ever had a situation where you just *happened* to be at the right place at the right time to help someone out? We've all heard stories where someone, for an unknown reason, reached out to a person or felt a tug in the heart to do something and it made a remarkable difference for someone's life. For example, there was a student who noticed a homeless teen in a Dunkin Donuts shop. The student felt like he should talk to this teen. He bought him a bagel and coffee and kept talking to him. By the end of the conversation, as he left, the teen handed him a note saying, "I was going to kill myself, but because of you, I don't want to anymore."

That student was a secondhand blessing from God. He was put in that restaurant at that specific time and felt compelled to talk and comfort this teen in a way he needed. What if he had blown this feeling off? What if he didn't care enough to follow through? Sometimes the smallest actions can mean the most to someone. We never know what someone is going through, but God does.

I love this verse from Ephesians 2:10, "For we are God's masterpiece. He has created us anew in Christ Jesus, so we can do the good things he planned for us long ago." Before you were born, God knew what gifts and talents he was going to give you and which ones you would develop. He knew the good and bad choices you would make and the consequences of those choices. He fully plans to use his chosen people to be a part of his master plan. What an honor we have to be a part of his work.

God not only gives us a variety of spiritual gifts, but he also intends for us to use them. When Jesus was asked in Matthew 22:37 about God's greatest commands, he replied, "You must love the Lord your God with all your heart, all your soul, and all your mind. This is the first and greatest command. A second is equally important: Love your neighbor as yourself. The entire law and all the demands of the prophets are based on these two commands."

What does this have to do with spreading kindness? Kindness is caring. It is showing your love for fellow human beings. God wants us to love him and to love others. We can show our love to him by loving others. Pastor Rick Warren of Saddleback Church and author of *The Purpose-Driven Life* gave a sermon back in 2015 about fulfilling our purpose here on earth by learning how to love God and others.

He shared that there are four ways to do this. Each way is gradually more challenging to accomplish. The first way to show love is to care for your own family. Many of us do dedicate a lot of our time and energy to those closest to us. This can be in the form of providing for your spouse and children in practical ways. We make sure there is food to eat and a safe, clean place to live. It also means giving your time, love, and attention to them. Most of us probably do pretty well on this first act of love. Our own family is a natural priority.

Now buckle your seat belt. This next part is not easy. The second way we need to show love is to treat other people as your family. This doesn't come as naturally. Why does he want us to do this? He wants others to know that Christians are known for their love. Galatians 6:10 tells us, "Therefore, whenever we have the opportunity, we should do good to everyone—especially to those in the family of faith."

There are many ways we can show others our love for them. Just as we show our family love by providing practical needs, we can share our resources with other believers. One big act of love is to sponsor a child or family in another country to help with their daily living expenses. I take the girls to a lot of Christian concerts. Many times, the band members will pause from their music to talk about organizations such as Food for the Hungry or World Vision. These are mission groups who organize ways to give to the needy in other countries across the world.

We have never been to Africa to see the poor conditions many families live in, firsthand. As an act of love though, we sponsor several girls there. This is an opportunity to help those in need but also to teach compassion to our own daughters. When they see the photos and receive the letters from these African girls, they are looking at the lives of people their own ages but with much less. Despite all of their struggles, they have a joy in them and a love for the Lord. This is so inspiring for all of us to witness.

To read about a girl excited about a goat her family received or to have a well dug in their village less than a mile away puts life into perspective. It helps us remember how very blessed we are and that we need to be good stewards of our blessings by sharing them with others.

My oldest daughter, Emily, is on a mission trip right now in Los Angeles. She and some fellow college students are serving the homeless on Skid Row. It has been an eye-opening experience for her. Our little rural town doesn't have homeless camps or people out in the open, begging in the streets. She has been helping in the soup kitchens and food pantries. She's handing out meals and sharing the Word as she is able. Her heart is to shine a light for Jesus and give these people hope.

There are all kinds of ways you can help others with practical needs locally too. If you hear of a single mom at your church who is struggling financially, you could help out with her bills. You can show love with your time by watching her kids. Maybe you have an elderly neighbor who could use help with yard work or cleaning the house. These are ways we can show love to others as we would our own families.

Jesus demonstrated this earlier in John 13 when he washed the feet of his disciples. He said in verses 14–17, "And since I, your Lord and Teacher, have washed your feet, you ought to wash each other's feet. I have given you an example to follow. Do as I have done to you. I tell you the truth, slaves are not greater than their master. Nor is the messenger more important than the one who sends the message. Now that you know these things, God will bless you for doing them."

If you hold a role of supervisor or manager over other employees, in what ways can you "wash your workers' feet?" How could you show them that you are not above them? That you care about them as God's children not just because they make money or provide a service for the business you lead?

Another biblical example of helping our neighbors is through the parable of the Good Samaritan. In Luke 10:30–37, Jesus tells the story of a man who was beaten, robbed, and left for dead by the side of a road. Sadly, a priest and a temple assistant passed right by him but did nothing to help. A Samaritan came by though, tended to the man's wounds, and took him to an inn. He even paid for his stay. Jesus teaches through this story and asks the question, "Now which of these three would you say was a neighbor to the man who was attacked?" Of course, we all know it was the Samaritan. No matter what our differences are, we should help our neighbors in need. Jesus tells us, "Now go and do the same."

The third way Pastor Rick says we should love others is to see their pain, even when you are in pain. In other words, if you have the flu, are you still thinking of others and ways you can bless them? Or are you solely focused on getting yourself better and hoping someone will serve *you*?

Think of the ultimate example of this. When Jesus was on the cross, in incredible pain, his thoughts were not on his own suffering. He asked God to forgive the criminals beside him. He told his mom that his disciple, John, would take care of her. He was still tending to the needs of others in his greatest pain.

In the classroom, there are many times when I have had a student misbehaving or causing a distraction. Maybe the student is complaining or refusing to do work. I need to set aside the discomfort and anxiety the student may be causing *me* and figure out where the pain is coming from. I'm often shocked when I pull a student aside to talk about some poor decisions being made.

One year I had a girl burst into tears when I asked her why she was yelling at her classmates. She said her dad was taken to jail for beating up her mom. Her sister cried herself to sleep at night, and she wasn't getting any sleep. Instead of punishing this girl who was making a lot of bad choices in the classroom, I told her I would pray for her and asked the counselor to help me get some resources in place for her.

It's easy to automatically come to the conclusion that people are just mean when they are honking in traffic or rude on the phone. There is usually some underlying pain or upset in their lives that we don't know about. I'm sure you've heard the saying, "What would Jesus do?" In these cases, we can ask ourselves this question and see if there is a way to meet the other people's needs. How could we comfort them or show his love and compassion instead of reacting in anger or retribution?

The fourth way that we can love others is to meet their needs even when our own needs aren't being met. Let's say you can barely afford your own bills, but you hear about a person in your church who can't afford the utility bill after a medical emergency. When you help that person in a time of need, despite your own needs, you are showing that person love. This is especially true in cases where you know the person may never be able to pay you back.

In Galatians 6:2–3 we are told, "Share each other's burdens, and in this way obey the law of Christ. If you think you are too important to help someone, you are only fooling yourself. You are not that important." Ouch. This is what is meant by loving others as yourself. Sometimes we have to put our own needs aside to serve those in the same or greater need.

The Scriptures teach that the proof of God's presence within our lives is our willingness to share his love with humanity. The earthly badge of our heavenly citizenship is our love relationship with others. A life of love is a deliberate choice on our part. We must choose this lifestyle against our natural bent for self-centeredness.

We know how God calls us to give; we need to be doers, not merely hearers of his Word. It is clearly spelled out in Matthew 7:26, "But anyone who hears my teaching and doesn't obey it is foolish, like a person who builds a house on sand."

With the Holy Spirit's help, our new life of love becomes a natural behavior. Then the emotional feelings of inner fulfillment follow. Responding to the needs of others shouldn't be a duty; rather it should be a privilege of normal Christian living. Our love in action can bring hope and joy to other Christians and even show nonbelievers that we are Christians not only in name but in deed as well. When we see an opportunity to serve others, we should see it as an honor to help hand out some wonderful secondhand blessings.

Prayer

> Lord, we know that no matter how long we've walked with you, we'll never be able to love like you or be like you without your help. We ask that you fill us with your Holy Spirit so that we may act through your power for your glory. Help us to give in the ways you call us to give and serve in the ways you call us to serve.

Reflection

1. How can you practically show kindness to those in your own home?

2. What are some examples of how you can treat other believers as you would treat your own family?

3. How can we be more mindful and helpful to others in pain even when we are in pain?

4. How does it strengthen our own faith when we are able to help someone in need when we are in need of the same thing?

CHAPTER 7

Giving God the Glory

Matthew 6:1–2: "Watch out! Don't do your good deeds publicly, to be admired by others, for you will lose the reward from your Father in heaven. When you give to someone in need, don't do as the hypocrites do-blowing trumpets in the synagogues and streets to call attention to their acts of charity! I tell you the truth, they have received all the reward they will ever get."

There are many passages in the Bible that teach us about our rewards. The thing to remember is that our true rewards await us in heaven. My family goes to Gull Lake Family Ministry Camp in Michigan each summer. The Scripture focus one summer was Matthew 6:19–21: "Don't store up treasures here on earth, where moths eat them, and where thieves break in and steal. Store your treasures in heaven, where moths and rust cannot destroy, and thieves do not break in and steal. Wherever your treasure is, there the desires of your heart will also be."

This is an example of Jesus teaching us about what we should value while here on earth. If we seek tangible praise or possessions, it won't last or be as meaningful as the rewards we will receive in heaven. If we do a kindness to seek an award or praise, we are not doing it to be more like Christ, we are doing to it receive appraisal now, from *this* world.

We see what we are supposed to do in 1 Timothy 6:19: "By doing this, they will be storing up their treasure as a good foundation for the future so that they may experience true life."

I want to be sure this doesn't come across as *earning* your way to heaven. The reward for our good deeds is *not* salvation. Ephesians 2:8–10 tells us very clearly: "God saved you by his grace when you believed. And you can't take credit for this; it is a gift from God. Salvation is not a reward for the good things we have done, so none of us can boast about it. For we are God's masterpiece. He has created us anew in Christ Jesus, so we can do the good things he planned for us long ago."

I started a Facebook group called A Deed a Day on the ninth anniversary of the month we started the diary. (You are ALL invited to join, by the way.) With so much negativity on social media and the news, I wanted to create a space for people to read about wonderful things that are happening all around us. By sharing our blessings with others, it inspires us to seek opportunities to serve and do what is right.

There are hundreds of people in the group, and posts are shared daily about kind things that people do. It's a joy to see how people are serving others. Some people find uplifting videos or post quotes about kindness. Encouraging verses are shared and stories of compassion as well.

When I first started the group, I was hesitant, wondering if people would use it as a spot to brag about something they did. As I explained earlier, Matthew 6:3 tells us that we are to "give our gifts in private, and your Father, who sees everything, will reward you." The reward should not be praise on Facebook. You'll receive much better satisfaction from the rewards from God.

I'm happy to say that people are sharing wonderful, encouraging stories and not seeking glory or praise at all. We are all encouraged by each other to continue to be more Christ-like. Galatians 1:10 says it well, "Obviously, I'm not trying to win the approval of people, but of God. If pleasing people were my goal, I would not be Christ's servant."

One more verse that comes to mind when we examine doing works for God's glory is found in John 14:12a, "I tell you the truth, anyone who believes in me will do the same works I have done." That seems like a tall order, considering that by this time, Jesus had walked on water, healed a blind man, fed five thousand people on five loaves and two fish, and turned water into wine!

Thankfully, this doesn't mean God expects us to perform miracles as amazing as these for our good works. We can take this to mean that people believe in Jesus on account of his works so those who do works and also believe may lead others to believe through their works. In simpler terms, your works should point people to Jesus. Or as Max Lucado explains it, "When you extend hospitality to others, you're not trying to impress people, you're trying to reflect God to them." (Redefining Beautiful, p. 63, 2009.)

My favorite compliment I have received is when people tell me that they see Christ's light shining through me. I've had this happen with people who know me well and with people I have just met. The first few times, I was surprised to hear this. I didn't realize how much I shared in casual conversation or that it struck others enough to point it out. I'm happy to know that people see my heart and that they see Jesus in there.

We need to always be pointing others to Jesus. We need to share his good news. Doing an act of kindness for the sake of being praised or thanked is like taking credit for the gifts God gave us. If we were camping and I found a glorious waterfall and brought you back a cup of water from it but didn't share where I got it or let you experience the waterfall for yourself, I'm not giving you the full gift! Sharing the cup of water *and* walking you over to the source would be a much richer blessing.

One example I can share is when Maddie had a tug on her heart to help others learn about Christ. Maddie really saw needs and wanted to do something about them. She had a boldness of faith that inspired me and others. I remember the day she came down to my classroom and asked, "Hey, did you know that some kids don't have a Bible?"

"Well, I'm sure there are some. Why do you ask?" I said.

"At recess, Ian said he didn't go to church. I asked him if he had a Bible at home, and he said he didn't. Then I asked him if he knew who Jesus was and he said he wasn't sure! I thought everyone knew about him."

"Well, hon, some kids have parents who don't go to church, so I guess they may not know Jesus. My family didn't go very often."

"Can we get him a Bible? He was asking a bunch of questions," she pleaded.

I hesitated. As a public-school teacher, I wondered, *Would she get in trouble doing this at school? Would I get in trouble?* I felt that familiar pull on my heart.

"Sure we can. That's a great idea," I said.

That night, after dinner, I found a kid-version study Bible for Maddie to give to the boy she talked to on recess. I was so proud of her for caring about the boy's faith and reaching out to him. What happened the next day was even better.

I was packing up my classroom after school and Maddie came bounding into my room. "Mom, can we get a couple more Bibles? When I gave Ian the Bible on recess, some other kids said they didn't have one. Could we get some for them?

I smiled and turned toward Maddie. "Who was asking for them this time?"

"Cassie and Allie." Cassie has never been to church. Allie has a couple times. But neither of them know anything about the Bible or Jesus, really."

"Well, I'm sure we can get some more Bibles. What did Ian say about the Bible you gave him?"

"He said thank you and seemed excited to have it. I told him I would teach him some stuff tomorrow if he brings it back out on recess."

That night, I told Matt about Maddie's evangelical efforts. He just smiled. When we made our way to Maddie's room to tuck her in, she had a bunch of questions for us. I wasn't sure how to answer all of them.

What happened the next morning blew me away. Maddie gathered her things for school and handed me a piece of folded paper. "Can you make five copies of this when we get to school?"

"What is it?" I asked.

"Well, I'm going to have a little Bible lesson at recess for the kids who are learning about the Bible. I looked up some of the stories that they may have at least heard of, like Noah's Ark and Christmas and Easter. I wrote down which books of the Bible they are in, and I'm going to teach them how to find them."

I unfolded the paper. There, in her penciled handwriting, was just as she said. *If you want to learn about Noah's Ark and all of the animals, they're in Genesis, the first book.* I couldn't believe it. I was too chicken, as a grown adult and teacher, to teach any kind of Bible lesson, and here was my eight-year-old creating lessons on her own to lead a group of kids at recess. I was speechless. My heart and eyes filled up.

Maddie led this group of kids under a tree on recess for several weeks. The most touching event was the day the class bully, Jessie, actually came to Maddie in tears. He shared that his little brother was in the hospital and asked Maddie to pray for him. Maddie ended up getting Jessie a Bible too. Not only that, but Jessie started being nicer to everyone in class. He later told Maddie that he had never prayed before that day.

We also enjoyed meaningful conversations about this kind of deed as a great example of giving God the glory. She was serving as God's hands and feet while obeying his command to share his love with others. The best part was, it didn't even occur to her to share this as a kind deed to record. We had been so intentional about noticing needs and learning to have compassion that she naturally *wanted* to do this because she saw a need and wanted to help.

This has thankfully become a part of who Maddie is. When you see her sing in the praise band, you see her love for Jesus. She is not performing but rather praising. When there is a child or animal in need, she can't help but care and want to help. Let's just say she has rescued a LOT of animals over the years and continues to do so.

She will spend every cent she has to help a friend going through a hard time by buying that person a special gift. She will stay up at night to talk to a classmate when her parents are fighting. If there is an amber alert on her phone for a missing child, she is following the story in tears until the child is found. Her heart seeks to give and to love.

When we go to visit elderly residents in the care center, she will stop to pray with them. She will hug them and hold their hands. She sings to them and shows them unconditional love. She doesn't do any of these things for praise or thanks. She does it as an extension of the love Jesus has for her. God gets the glory as she shares how Jesus loves these people.

These acts of kindness that Maddie does are still rewarding while here on earth. I don't want people to feel guilty about enjoying their giving and serving opportunities. We can receive wonderful feelings of contentment and purpose for our gifts to others and still be rewarded in heaven. Randy Alcorn, author of *Giving Is the Good Life,* says that it's not just "someday our giving will bring us good. It will actually do us good here and now—at the same time it does good for others."

As long as we are giving God the glory, we can get excited about how our giving changes others' lives as it changes our own. God moves us to do all kinds of things for people. They can be done in secret, and you can still experience great joy in knowing you made a difference.

There are times I've paid for students' lunch accounts when I knew their families were going through hard times. At our school, after so many dollars in debt, you no longer receive the standard school lunch; you have to eat a government-issued cheese sandwich. Everyone knows what that means when you get the cheese sandwich. It is embarrassing for the child, who is already probably going through rough circumstances at home. It isn't the child's fault that the parents cannot afford to pay the bills. It isn't the child's fault that the parents didn't fill out the paperwork to be registered to receive free or reduced-cost lunches.

We have something called Buddy Bags that go home with students each Friday. They are filled with nonperishable food items that are meant to help out families with meals over the weekends. These go home to families based on a questionnaire sent home at the beginning of the year. If parents give consent to receive them, they get them every week. Friday afternoons, the announcement is made for kids to come and get their Buddy Bags from the office. Every Friday, I personally get the bag for my students and place it in their lockers or book bag before that announcement, when no one will see. It is just a little thing, but it saves kids any embarrassment or teasing. It gives me great joy to do this for them.

Praying for others is another way we can do something meaningful for others without them even knowing about it. We have a prayer board on our refrigerator. We add names to it as we hear of situations needing prayer. The kitchen is a hub in our home, so we see those names throughout the day, and it reminds us to pray for them often. It's definitely OK to let people know you are praying for them too. It may give them great encouragement to know they are being thought of and that God will hear from more than just them.

When we pray for others or give in private, although the recipients don't always know, God does. Sometimes it is important to give openly too. This allows us to get God into the conversation! When we give something to someone and tell them we felt a nudge to bless them or that God was laying a burden on your heart to do something to show his love, you are not only helping the person with the gift but also praising and glorifying God in the process. This could lead to questions or curiosity about your faith from the person that could even lead to a saving knowledge of him or a stronger relationship.

Prayer

> Lord, thank you for my salvation. I pray that those who feel they can earn their way to heaven through good works would understand our works aren't what get us there. I pray that they would know that they need to truly believe that it is only through Jesus we can be saved because he died to save us all from our sins. Help us to continue to do good works as an outpouring of our desire to show Christ's love. Help us to spread joy and experience joy as we give in your name.

Reflection

1. What ways could you share that the only way to heaven is through a saving knowledge of Jesus?

2. How do you show your faith through your good works?

3. In what ways do you praise God when good things happen to you?

4. Read Proverbs 19:17: "If you help the poor, you are lending to the Lord-and he will repay you!" What does this mean? How does it relate to what the Bible says Jesus will do when he comes in his glory with the angels? Matthew 25:40 says, "And the King will say, 'I tell you the truth, when you did it to one of the least of these my brothers and sisters, you were doing it to me.'"

CHAPTER 8

Having an Impact

Since God chose you to be the holy people he loves, you must clothe yourselves with tenderhearted mercy, kindness, humility, gentleness, and patience. Make allowance for each other's faults, and forgive anyone who offends you. Remember, the Lord forgave you, so you must forgive others. Above all, clothe yourselves with love, which binds us all together in perfect harmony. And let the peace that comes from Christ rule in your hearts. For as members of one body, you are called to live in peace. And always be thankful. Let the message about Christ, in all its richness, fill your lives. Teach and counsel each other with all the wisdom he gives. Sing psalms and hymns and spiritual songs to God with thankful hearts. And whatever you do or say, do it as a representative of the Lord Jesus, giving him thanks through him to God the Father. (Colossians 3:12–17)

I know the above passage is long, but isn't it SO good? Isn't this the reason we perform acts of kindness—as an overflow of our hearts because we are secure in Christ's love?

My family hit some dry spells along the way while trying to serve others, especially over the summer. Thankfully, God is patient and merciful. We celebrated a year of intentional acts of kindness because of this.

Have you ever watched the video "Bully a Plant" made by IKEA about the effects of kindness and cruelty on houseplants? Employees of IKEA took two large, healthy houseplants and placed them in a school for thirty days. They gave them equal treatment as far as the amount of sunlight and watering. The difference was that one of the plants was subjected to compliments and encouragement on a regular basis, and the other was verbally abused. People recorded and played positive things like, "You're making a difference in the world," and "you're beautiful," for one plant. People recorded and played unkind things to the other plant like, "You're useless," and "nobody likes you."

The plant that was treated unkindly was noticeably different at the end of thirty days. It was wilted and looked unhealthy. The plant treated with kindness was healthy and beautiful. There are doubters who say they must have done other things to cause this to happen. Maybe someone put something bad in the soil of the mistreated plant or gave extra nutrients to the healthy plant? We could say the same thing about people, couldn't we? We could try to explain away the positive and negative effects of how we treat others.

A fourth grader at my school decided to test this experiment for his science fair project this year. He used self-watering oregano seed kits. He spent two minutes, twice a day, saying kind or mean things to each plant for three weeks. The plant that was treated kindly sprouted and flourished. The plant that was told unkind things barely sprouted out of the soil.

If even a plant can experience these effects, what major difference can we make by using kind words with people? It doesn't take much time or effort to give a compliment or say an encouraging word. We can all make a difference by being kind to people to help them flourish and grow.

The goal from the very beginning was to be less selfish and think of others more. This grew into something much more meaningful and spiritual, through God's grace. We went from always wondering what the day would bring for us to what we could do for someone else in the day. It changed our whole outlook on life and grew our faith.

Who would have thought that trying to do a simple kind act a day would be so personally rewarding? I feel like my family better understands the joy of giving rather than seeking to receive. We are the blessed recipients of Christ's love and that makes us want to share his love with others.

One way this project grew and made a bigger impact spun off of Maddie's Bible study on recess. Her little Bible study is what led to the start of the Fellowship of Christian Students (FCS) at our school. I would have never guessed that God would equip me with the courage to lead a group of young believers. I'll give you a little background.

I can say without a doubt that God called me from a very young age to follow him. My family rarely went to church, but I went to Sunday school and youth group on Wednesday nights when I could. I remember asking neighbors and grandparents for rides to church. I felt the desire to go. I didn't know much about the Bible, but I just believed. I even "played" church at home.

When I finally got my driver's license, I drove myself to church. Even going off to college, one of my priorities was to find a church to attend. One summer, I lived with my aunt in Texas. Even then, I found a church to attend. (Keep in mind, this was before the days of GPS, and I'm directionally challenged. It was a big deal for this little country mouse to find her way in the big city by herself!) I can't explain this pull I had or why I prayed so frequently, but I'm thankful God gave me the gift of the Holy Spirit.

My husband and I looked for a mutual church home while we were dating. Each Sunday, we visited a different church until we narrowed it down to the one we felt most comfortable in. With Matt's work schedule, his attendance was sporadic, but we went when we could. (He was a police officer on the night shift and worked every other weekend.) We ended up getting married in that church, so even though we don't attend there anymore, it is still a special place.

Fast forward to the birth of our daughters. Faith was now an even bigger priority. We attended church regularly, listened to Christian music, had the girls dedicated in our church, and sent them to Christian preschools. Maddie and Emily went to vacation Bible schools in the summers and Wednesday night youth groups. I wanted them to have more opportunities to learn than I did. They had more Bible verses memorized in elementary school than I knew as an adult.

In many ways, the girls guided *our* path more than we guided theirs. From praying for our food at meals, to helping them memorize Scriptures for youth group, they led in ways we hadn't. I was afraid to do any leading in church. I didn't want to teach Sunday school or youth group for fear I would be found out that I didn't know much about the Bible. I was afraid a child would ask something that I didn't know how to answer or I would say the wrong thing. What if kids saw that I didn't know much about the Bible as a grown adult and thought it wasn't important? I know when I was in high school and other adults told me they didn't know how to do Algebra, I drew the conclusion that it must not be that important in life if it is forgotten so easily.

The story I told myself was that I was much better suited rocking babies in the nursery, playing the keyboard in the praise band, and helping with breakfast setup at church. I thought that I should just stay out of the way of the people who know Scripture better and allow them to teach the little kids in Sunday school and on Wednesday nights.

That all changed when Maddie's faith-filled determination to spread God's Word in elementary school inspired me to start a Christian group at our school. Yes, in our *public* school! Have you ever heard anyone say that it seemed like God was telling them to do something? Well, I felt it. I couldn't stop thinking about it. I finally told God I would try.

There was already a Fellowship of Christian Athletes (FCA) club at the middle and high school levels. I wrote up a proposal to start an FCS club at the elementary grade levels, with me as their leader. It just seemed like we needed to reach the kids in elementary school to have them learn about Jesus at an early age. Having Jesus in your heart as you grow up can make life so much better!

Maddie was noticing kids who wanted to know more about Jesus. Maybe if we could teach them a little about him, they would spread what they learned to their families too. God's hand was in every step of the way. I was approved to have the club, as long as it took place before or after school hours, not during school. I started spreading the word about our club through church youth groups in town. I had parents asking if they could bring breakfast snacks. I designed T-shirts, found someone to lead a song each time, and searched for lessons that I could learn ahead of the kids for each meeting.

Now I know it doesn't seem as powerful to reach out to kids who already attend a church or youth group, but God had a plan. The power in getting many believers gathered together in fellowship is reaffirming to those attending. The way it spread though was through these awesome kids wearing their shirts boldly (They had verses on the backs of them and FCS on the fronts of them), happily coming out of my room in the morning, and talking about what they learned.

When you are excited to be a part of something special, you naturally want to share it. That is exactly what these kids did. It was only a matter of time when I was having parents reach out asking if their kids could be a part of the group even if they didn't attend church. How amazing is that? Kids started coming because their friends were inviting them or they were curious or they saw the joy our FCS kids were experiencing. That's God's love in action.

In our elementary school, we have a little over three hundred students. We have had the club for many years now and average sixty kids each time. That's a good portion of the student population! They even have to wake up an hour early to get to school for the seven o'clock in the morning meetings. It is a wonderful hour of prayer, worship, learning, and fellowship. I have even had some of the now middle and high school kids come back to visit on occasion. It's the biggest club in our school.

I can't tell you how inspiring it is to have kids from all walks of life come to my room to learn more about Jesus. Some go to church regularly, and some were like me and didn't know very much. Some had their first exposure right in my classroom. This was proof to me that God doesn't always call the equipped, but he equips those he calls.

This further inspired me to join a Bible study group and learn more. One of my running friends was leading a Bible study at his home, and I asked if I could start coming. It was in this first Bible study group that I fully understood salvation and gave my heart to Christ. I couldn't believe that all my life I thought I understood what it meant to live for Christ and have eternal salvation. I just thought you had to believe he existed. I had believed that for as long as I could remember!

I didn't realize that I needed to repent and truly understand that his death on the cross was to save us from our sins so we could be right with God. Since that time, I've been involved in many Bible studies with small groups, large groups, and one-on-one formats. I've been baptized and go to ladies' Bible conferences and events. I'm even keynoting at ladies' day events for churches. Who would have ever thought that? Not me. To be writing this book right now is surreal.

My faith has never been stronger. I know that I still have plenty of room to grow. Thank God for that. I'm still learning from the Bible and from those further along on their faith journeys than me.

The ripple continues though. Through me learning about salvation and giving my heart to Jesus, my husband was seeing a change in me. He started to become more involved at our church. This is a big deal.

Matt grew up in a home where church was a regular Sunday routine. When we were dating, he actually said at one point, "I was forced to go to church when I was a kid, and I don't want to be forced to go to church as an adult." I remember I was crushed, thinking I may have made a huge mistake with this relationship.

He came around though. We visited several churches until he found the one he was most comfortable in. We ended up dating two years, were engaged for a year, then got married in that very church, just down the street from our first house.

As I mentioned before, Matt is a police officer. When we were first married, he was on the night shift. His sleep schedule made it hard to get up each Sunday to attend. We actually went through some marital struggles after having our daughters when he resisted going to church. After some Christian counseling, we made it through and recommitted to have a Christian home.

I had an incredible hunger to keep learning and growing my faith. I remember I was nervous to tell Matt I wanted to be baptized. (He and I were both baptized as babies.) I explained to him that I wanted to do it as an outward expression of my faith. My parents chose for me the first time, but I wanted to obey God and do it for *me* this time. I thought he would think I was crazy.

I remember bringing it up one morning casually as we were getting ready for work. He didn't say much at first, then surprised me and said he wanted to be baptized too.

After several weeks of classes with our pastor, we were ready for the big day. We invited our families and friends and drove out to a pond, where several other members of our church were going to be baptized as well. We each had to stand at the microphone and share our testimony. Matt became emotional as he shared his. I could tell God was stirring his heart. I was proud to be able to do this in front of our girls. It was very special to do this important act of faith together.

From that point, Matt started going to a monthly men's Saturday group study, an adult Bible study with small groups at our church, and went with a group of men from our church to help out when the horrible tornado happened in Joplin, Missouri. He even stood up in front of our church to share a testimony when he returned from Joplin.

I would have never guessed that he would grow in so many ways, after seeming resistant to the idea of church in the beginning of our relationship. I'm so glad God worked in his heart. When Maddie was baptized last summer at church camp, Matt and the pastor there got to baptize her together. What a special memory for both of them.

This year, when I had a speaker for my FCS group cancel on me, I half-jokingly asked Matt if he wanted to fill in. He accepted. That made me a bit nervous. What would he say? This wasn't in his comfort zone.

He brought in his SWAT gear and talked to the kids about Ephesians 6:13–14, "Therefore, put on every piece of God's armor so you will be able to resist the enemy in the time of evil. Then after the battle you will still be standing firm. Stand your ground, putting on the belt of truth and the body armor of God's righteousness."

Sharing about the armor of God, he went through each of his items: his shield, belt, and helmet. Matt showed the kids a patch he bought for his bulletproof vest with that verse on it. He explained what the passage meant and how it helped him when he was on a dangerous call. He talked about praying with the SWAT team before entering a building. Most importantly, he explained that he doesn't have to have fear because God doesn't give us a spirit of fear. God's plans are already made, and whatever his will may be is what should happen in each situation.

I was so impressed and proud of my man, standing in front of a room of sixty kids, sharing his heart for God. What a blessing to me and to all of the kids.

With Matt's faith and my faith growing, we naturally wanted the faith of our girls to be growing as well.

When Emily was a baby, the theme for Emily's nursery room was Noah's Ark, and we had her dedicated in our church on Mother's Day when she was one month old. I remember singing her "Amazing Grace" as I'd nurse her and rock her at night. I wanted Emily to grow up in a home knowing who Jesus was and having a strong faith.

Emily went to a Christian preschool, and we took her to church and youth group regularly. It was a priority. Thankfully, we have always had wonderful teachers in all of those classes. She had a strong, child-like faith—as in, she had never known any other way.

There was one area of her life, however, where she needed to grow. She had anxiety. Maybe it was something about being the firstborn; maybe it was that we were too protective; maybe it was related to not having a strong enough faith yet; but it was real.

When it came to spending the night at a friend's house, we would get a call to come and get her. She got to the point that she would make up excuses to not even go in the first place. If there was a slumber party invite, she was suddenly not feeling well. When we finally caught on to this, we worried that she would stop getting invited.

She was also deathly afraid of anyone in a costume, storms, and the possibility of something happening to us if we were gone. We aren't sure where all of these fears came from, but we knew it was preventing her from participating in many opportunities. For example, she was selected to attend a leadership camp, had the chance to go to a swim camp, had many slumber party invitations, and ultimately turned them all down.

It was during her fifth-grade year that we started the Deed Diary. Since that time, she had felt the pull we all did to be Christ's hands and feet and also witnessed our growing commitment to Christian living. We felt like the best way to deal with her anxieties was to handle it from a biblical standpoint. She needed to learn to trust Jesus and be anxious for nothing. Second Timothy 1:7 says, "For God has not given us a spirit of fear and timidity, but of power, love, and self-discipline." We had her meet with our pastor several times to talk about her fears and pray with him.

One summer, when she was in middle school, we met with our pastor and decided we needed to dish out some tough love. Emily was very close with our pastor, PJ, and his wife Lora. (She was her youth leader.) We invited them over to help us deliver the news that we had signed her up to go to a weeklong ministry camp in Michigan.

Emily was completely caught off guard the day PJ and Lora came over. She gave them both a big hug and figured they were there for a visit or dinner. Emily sat on the loveseat, next to me; PJ and Lora were on the couch across from us; Matt was in an armchair in the corner of the room. PJ started us out, talking about the camp. He shared what he and his family loved about it. He also talked about how much Matt and I loved her and wanted what was best for her.

Emily started putting the pieces together and squirmed a bit. She grabbed the pillow from behind her and started to curl into a fetal position, scooting away from me. By the time PJ turned it over to us to tell her she was going, she was in tears.

PJ traded spots with me and tried to talk with her a bit. He told her he wanted to meet with her a few times leading up to the trip. He also said he wanted her to memorize 2 Timothy 1:7, then he would take her to Dairy Queen for a blizzard.

We all prayed together, and when PJ and Lora left, Emily walked directly to her room without a word, and shut the door. I wasn't used to seeing her like this. I suppose, in fairness, she wasn't used to us handling her fears in this way either.

We gave her over an hour to process before we came in to talk to her. She wasn't very interested in talking and felt betrayed. It was a rough few weeks leading up to the day she left for camp.

I'm thankful that I had to leave for a writing conference in Los Angeles the day before she needed to go. It would have been really hard to see her break down on the day she was dropped off at her youth leader's house. It was also good that I was so far away and couldn't come and get her from Michigan if she called, begging to come back home.

We were able to get special permission to let her use a phone if she wanted to call home. We gave it to her youth leader, who was staying in the same cottage as her and her friends. I was ready for a desperate call the first night, but it didn't come. I can't tell you all of the thoughts that went through my head. I felt like a terrible mom, forcing her to go. Maybe she just needed to mature? Would she resent us or not trust us now? What's wrong with her not wanting to leave home?

The next day, I checked my phone all day. Nothing. I finally called her youth leader.

"Heather? Is Emmy OK?" I asked.

"Shannon, you wouldn't believe it. She was so tired from all of the activities yesterday. We got back here and everyone crashed. She didn't even ask to call."

"You mean, she slept through the night and didn't wake you or get scared?"

"Nope, and she's having a great time." Heather laughed.

I could hear the girls in the background. My eyes were filling. I couldn't believe it. Answered prayers. *Thank you, God.*

"Do you want to talk to her real quick?" Heather asked, after my long pause.

"Yes! Put her on, please."

"Hi, Mom!" Emily said, as if she didn't have a care in the world.

"Hi, honey! I'm so glad you're having a good time! I'm so happy for you!"

"Well, I am. It's a lot of fun here, and my camp counselor is awesome. Her name is Nancy Brew! I'll tell you all about it when I get home."

"I can't wait to hear. I love you so much, Em. Bye."

I returned from my trip to LA before she got home from camp. As a surprise reward for her bravery, we set up a turtle tank in her room. (She had always wanted a turtle.) When I picked her up, I was so excited to hear all about her week and show her the turtle.

I figured she would be jumping up and down, excited when I saw her. That was not the case. She looked sad and disappointed. We got home, and she saw the turtle and smiled. I asked her what was wrong.

"Are you still upset with us for making you go? Was a week too long?" I asked.

"No, I'm sad because I wanted to stay longer. I can't describe why it was so good there. All of the counselors there, the kids, the leaders, the speakers—they were all so nice, and it was so peaceful. It was fun, but it just felt good to be around people who love Jesus."

Since that summer, Emily has been back every summer to that camp. We still go there now as a family. She also started staying over with friends sometimes.

Later that year after her first time going, she came home from youth group and prayed to Jesus for her salvation. I still remember her coming to me in tears and telling me all about it. The next summer, she was baptized. The summer after that, she surprised us all and signed up to go on a mission trip to a dangerous part of Mexico with a small group from our church. That one took Matt and me to our knees. We were worried about her safety, but of course, we didn't let her know that.

Throughout high school, she had a lonely walk. She was disappointed to find out that many of her friends were not Christians and many didn't share her same values when it came to making moral choices. She is happiest doing Bible studies with close friends or mentors, sharing encouraging verses throughout our home, and creating art.

Emily now attends Grace College and is studying to be an elementary teacher. She hopes to teach in a Christian school someday. She had a tough time living away from home and still comes back almost every weekend. Others have made comments like, "You need to make her stay on campus and experience college life," or "she must still be afraid to be away from home."

This girl has a strong faith and is experiencing college in a way that works for her. She gets to combine her career training with her home life. I couldn't be prouder. The day we had to move her into college was difficult for all of us. It's hard to say goodbye even when you know it is temporary. Here is what Emily said about her first year of school:

> My first year of college was an extremely tough experience for me. Living away from home was a big adjustment and the stress of schoolwork on top of that caused me to be even more out of my comfort zone. Without my faith in Jesus, I do not think that I could have handled it all. Waking up each morning to do my devotion to start out my day, attending chapel regularly, going to growth groups, and talking with others about God really helped me to grow in my faith and gave me the extra motivation to work hard in school, so I can live out my dream of being a teacher for the glory of God.

As I mentioned earlier, she's on her second mission trip now. This girl who was afraid to spend the night at a friend's house only five minutes away is now in a much "scarier" area of Los Angeles, serving others in ways that could fill a whole Deed Diary. She learned the power of her faith and shows her appreciation by blessing others with what she has been given.

You just never know what kinds of ripples will occur when you are throwing one of God's pebbles out into the world. When we celebrated our Deed Diary year milestone, I wanted to share this with more people. When you experience something this wonderful, you want to share it. Just like Christ's good news. It is SO good, you want to obey the Lord's teaching and teach and counsel each other with the wisdom he gives.

Since I love writing, I decided I would try to share our Deed a Day experience with the *Chicken Soup for the Soul* publishers. I wanted to share our blessings with a thankful heart. As the above passage says, we should be clothed in love. As members of one body, we can bond in the peace that kindness, patience, mercy, humility, and gentleness bring.

On August 18, 2011, I received an acceptance letter from the *Chicken Soup* publishers. They wanted to include my story in their book, *Chicken Soup for the Soul: Find Your Happiness.* My goal to encourage kindness was working. When the book released, I received emails from people all around the world sharing their Deed a Day Diary experiences. I was so touched that other families saw the value and perhaps would come to Christ as a result, if they weren't already saved.

Chicken Soup for the Soul ended up including the story in *Raising Great Kids* in 2015 and *Simply Happy* in 2016. I've had people contact me about writing for other similar anthologies on kindness after seeing the Deed a Day story. People with podcasts and blog posts began contacting me to find out more and ask about our experience. I never would have thought that the night no one would let the dog in would end up causing someone from another country to help other people too.

When I saw the impact intentional acts of kindness had on our family, I just had to try this in my classroom. When I told the kids about the idea, I showed them our Deed Diary. They seemed as excited as my girls were the first day they heard of the idea.

We kicked if off with writing thank-you notes to all of the staff. This included the school nurse, janitors, secretaries, cooks, bus drivers, assistants, specials teachers, and more. The kids were touched by seeing the librarian and other recipients hang up their notes with pride. Many came and thanked the kids personally.

While contemplating how this would look with over twenty kids, I thought it would be overwhelming to keep track of a deed a day for each child, every day. Instead, we committed to three kind acts a day for our whole classroom. You should have seen the kids scramble when someone accidentally dumped their crayons! They certainly delivered on their mission to do nice things for others.

I now teach third grade, and in addition to having the FCS club, I also have a Kindness Club. We do all sorts of things to promote kindness. We have written letters to those in the military, we've stuffed little plastic tubes with positive messages and hid them all over the school, we've done math-a-thons to raise money for children's hospitals, and we've held school-wide kindness challenges.

Kids from my classroom and throughout the school now come up with their own acts of kindness. We often see notes on lockers, or kids will hold toy drives or collect canned goods for the food pantry. Kindness is like a seed. Once it is planted, if nurtured, can grow into something beautiful. Some of my students raised money and collected donations for the animal shelter and police department. I got special permission from their parents to take them to deliver these special items in person.

I had a student who said her mom always put a love note in her lunchbox every day. She noticed that many kids didn't receive these. She spent a week of her recesses inside writing and decorating notes. The next week, we "broke" into lockers for every student, and if there was a lunch box, we put a kind note inside. I witnessed many happy and surprised faces in the cafeteria that week as kids opened their lunches and found them.

Another student of mine noticed a boy in our class who seemed to always get into trouble. (He had some anger and self-control issues he was working on.) The first boy saved up money to buy him a slinky toy to play with when he was feeling upset. He thought it would calm him. When I told him to go ahead and give it to him, he was a little scared to do so. He approached him and timidly handed it to him. The boy grabbed him and hugged him, with his head on his chest for several seconds, thanking him. It was a very touching scene.

While researching for this book, I asked people what acts of kindness have had the greatest impact on them. Most answered with ways others have served them in love. This ranged from providing transportation, to chopping wood, to bringing meals during a hard time. The reason it was so meaningful is because it was showing compassion. The recipient felt cared for. There were others listed that may have seemed insignificant, but they meant a lot to the person at the time. One person said she was having a horrible week and someone gave her a sucker and a card and that meant the world to her.

I love that when I asked people what kinds of good deeds they had done for others, they were very humble about it. Some people sent private messages or prefaced their sharing with the fact that they felt funny about sharing publicly what they did. This shows their true spirit of giving. They not only did something kind, but they did it to bless someone, not to receive accolades.

When people shared things they have done for others, they said things like, "It was really easy to do," or "it doesn't take much time to . . . " Most said they were happy to do what they did and would do it again. God loves a cheerful giver, and we all know the saying that it is better to give than to receive. How can you not feel good when you see the smile or gratitude of the recipient of your kindness?

Ephesians 2:10 says, "For we are his workmanship, created in Christ Jesus for good works, which God prepared beforehand so that we would walk in them." We never know when we are one of God's scheduled blessings for someone else. We may come up with an idea to make a card for someone and think it is a random act, but actually, God planned for you to do this right when the person needed it. You see, this book is about doing a deed a day, but really it isn't. It's about planting seeds, sowing seeds God plants in us, and loving others as he teaches us to love.

Although as a family we stopped recording in the Deed Diary after that year, the impact it has had on our lives and the lessons we learned will be with us forever. The impact it may have on others could be a ripple we can never measure. I pray that my own family will continue to spread kindness. Perhaps my sweet students who have done good deeds in class or in the Kindness Club will continue to do so. Those reading *Chicken Soup for the Soul*, taking part in the Deed a Day Facebook group, and even maybe reading this book may decide to spread a little more kindness. The reach will never be fully known.

Let us also remember the impact generosity can have on our own lives. Maya Angelou said, "When you get, give." Jesus says in Luke 6:38, "Give, and you will receive. Your gift will return to you in full—pressed down, shaken together to make room for more, running over, and poured into your lap. The amount you give will determine the amount you get back."

Although our motive for giving shouldn't be so we can get back, this does happen. We get back joy, blessings from God, and blessings from others when we extend kindness. We also get the honor of doing God's work here on earth for his glory.

In Matthew 25, we are told that Jesus will come and sit on his throne to separate his people. Verses 34–36 tell us:

> Then the King will say to those on his right, Come, you who are blessed by my Father, inherit the Kingdom prepared for you from the creation of the world. For I was hungry, and you fed me. I was thirsty, and you gave me a drink. I was a stranger, and you invited me into your home. I was naked, and you gave me clothing. I was sick, and you cared for me. I was in prison, and you visited me. His people will be confused, not understanding when they saw Jesus and did these things.

Jesus tells them in verse 40, "And the King will say, I tell you the truth, when you did it to one of the least of these my brothers and sisters, you were doing it to me."

When we show love for others, we really are showing love for Jesus and by Jesus. It impacts the giver and the receiver.

Prayer

> Lord, thank you for giving us your Holy Spirit. Continue to create a boldness in us to spread your Word and fulfill your purpose. I pray that many would heed your calling, choose to follow you, and strive to be your hands and feet for your glory.

Reflection

1. If God asked you, "What have you done with the gifts I gave you?" how would you answer?

2. How does showing kindness and spreading it to others show the love of Christ?

3. Read 2 Thessalonians 3:13: "As for the rest of you, dear brothers and sisters, never get tired of doing good." Have you ever felt tired of being the good guy when others may not treat you well? How do we conquer this feeling and maintain right living?

4. In what ways has serving others grown your faith or the faith of others?

CHAPTER 9

Why It's Hard

So we keep on praying for you, asking our God to enable you to live a life worthy of his call. May he give you the power to accomplish all the good things your faith prompts you to do. Then the name of our Lord Jesus will be honored because of the way you live, and you will be honored along with him. This is all made possible because of the grace of our God and Lord, Jesus Christ. (2 Thessalonians 1:11–12)

Deep down, we all want to love and be loved. The best use of our life is to love. So, why is it sometimes hard to extend kindness? Why doesn't it come naturally to treat others how we want to be treated? When it comes down to it, the real question to ponder is, why are we so self-focused?

Many times we don't seek to do good deeds on our own because we are sinful. We were born sinners, as humans. It's important to pray for the Holy Spirit to lead us, guide us, and direct us. Whether you have lived a rough or rich life, the desire to do what is pleasing to the Lord goes against our flesh nature. We have to keep our hearts in check. The struggle is real. Jesus reminds us in

Matthew 26:41, "Keep watch and pray, so that you will not give in to temptation. For the spirit is willing, but the body is weak!"

It is human nature to wake up in the morning and think about what you will make *yourself* for breakfast, what to pack *yourself* for lunch, decide what clothes *you'll* wear, run through what *you* want to get done that day, and go check off all of the boxes. There is nothing inherently wrong with this, but as Christ's hands and feet, we are called to be more and do more. We need to notice and interrupt our mindless patterns and seek ways to love others.

In the midst of writing this, the Coronavirus is wreaking havoc on our world. Even Christians are struggling in these times of panic and resorting to self-interest as they react in fear.

One of my students shared this week that he witnessed a fight in one of our local stores over a package of toilet paper. Another shared a similar story over a case of water bottles in yet another store. I have no idea if these people are Christians or not. It doesn't matter. The point is that the message our children are receiving is that when we are faced with fear, we panic and react selfishly and rudely.

I rarely listen to the news, but with the Coronavirus spreading, I've tried to stay in tune with what I need to know for the safety of my family and students. This week, I heard a weather reporter say, "There is a tornado threat later today to the south of us. This is good news. No threat in our area." I couldn't believe she said that. I don't think she meant to come across as being relieved that someone else is in danger of major destruction, but this comment was not a loving way to talk about our neighbors.

I've also heard many people dismiss the seriousness of the Coronavirus, claiming, "It just affects old people and those in bad health. The rest of us should be able to carry on as usual." This is in response to things like sporting event cancellations, school closures, and various postponements. Again, a response that doesn't really model much compassion for our fellow man.

It is more important than ever to be mindful of our sin nature and take a step back to reflect before we react. We need to educate ourselves with facts and with God's Word in these times rather than go into a "survival of the fittest" mode. We need to teach compassion and find examples of this that we can shine a light on. Mr. Rogers said we should "look for the helpers" in times of tragedy. What an awesome lesson for us to learn and pass on to our kids. There are always helpers. And better yet, we can *be* one of those helpers. What if our kids were able to witness the helpers more often and share those stories?

Pastor John C. Maxwell said, in his book, *Intentional Living*:

> When we live our lives intentionally for others, we begin to see the world through eyes other than our own, and that inspires us to do more than belong; we participate. We do more than care; we help. We go beyond being fair; we are kind. We go beyond dreaming; we work. Why: Because we want to make a difference. (p. 16, 2015)

How many times do we meet our own needs first, and if you have time or resources left over, you then offer your surplus? I'm guilty of this. I'm embarrassed to admit that when youth group kids have come around from time to time to collect food for the food pantry, I've dug through to see what wasn't being eaten. I found the cans and boxes in the back of the cabinet that no one in our house wanted. I didn't try to offer our best or something I needed for a recipe I was making the next day.

This has to be a conscious choice every day to try not to let sin control us. We are to be in prayer about what God's will is. As you try to be pleasing to God and love God, he will bless you. Remember, God chose you before you even decided to become saved. Colossians 3:12 tells us this, "Since God chose you to be the holy people he loves, you must clothe yourselves with tenderhearted mercy, kindness, humility, gentleness, and patience."

We need to show God's love to others and bless others in the process. It's not always easy to do because our natural tendency is to sin. This is another stage in our process to become holier. By showing God's love, we are pointing people to him. We are ambassadors for Christ. We have to represent our God, our Father, in a way that shows his character.

When our girls were younger, we would often tell them to be careful with their words and actions out in the world because they are representing our family. Especially with me being a teacher in the community and Matt being the police chief of our town, it is important that we are walking the walk and talking the talk. We cannot expect respect if we are not taking school seriously or if we are breaking the law.

If I get a speeding ticket in town or steal something, that is not going to look good. If the girls flunk a class at school, that is not reflecting our family values either. There is a big responsibility to be a good role model when you are trusted with the safety of the community and the education of our future generation. We cannot take that lightly.

As we became stronger in our faith, we realized this to a much higher degree. Our conversations became more about being a representative of the family of God, not just the Anderson family. If we claim to be Christians, we need to be careful about how we represent our family because of our Father's job. We need to show that we have respect and love for him so others will have respect too.

If I use the Lord's name in vain, gossip about people, dress in clothing that is revealing, tell lies, and start dealing drugs, then those around me will question my respect for my Father. They will wonder what I really believe in and stand for. Why would they want to take part in something that is not special enough to care about on a regular basis? Worse yet, what if they find themselves doing similar things because they trust your example as a Christian? Jesus warns us about this in Luke 17:1–3, "There will always be temptations to sin, but what sorrow awaits the person who does the tempting! It would be better to be thrown into the sea with a millstone hung around your neck than to cause one of these little ones to fall into sin. So watch yourselves!"

I can't be a hypocrite and wear a cross necklace and Christian sweatshirt, then curse someone out in the grocery store. Even with stress levels high with the Coronavirus pandemic, it is so important that I show Christian love. Fighting over the last roll of toilet paper on the shelves is not being a blessing to anyone. People would see that I don't really care about being a Christian when the times are hard. I just like the swag that goes with being a Christian. Or maybe someone just likes the label of being a Christian because people will think you are a nice person. This can harm the faith of others when we don't represent ourselves as true followers.

I tell my students they need to be role models and represent our school when we are out on field trips. If people see the name of our school on our bus and our shirts, they will associate our school with who we are and how we behave. If the kids leave a mess or are disrespectful, the people working at the establishment are going to think the kids that go to Van Elementary are a bunch of kids with no manners or respect. We have to show that we have pride in where we come from and care about our school enough to show it.

When we represent ourselves well, people grow to trust you and what you stand for. Represent Jesus and others will grow to trust him and what he stands for. When I see people blessing others, it inspires me to want to do the same. It also causes me to want to know them more. I want to know more about their lifestyle, what they read, what they listen to, what church they go to. People who have an inner joy and the desire to spread joy shine a light for Christ.

It's easy to be nice and wear a smile when we are surrounded by other Christian followers who are walking the walk. The struggle comes when we are around difficult people or are in a difficult situation. I remember when our oldest daughter came back from her first time at that weeklong church camp and she said, "At Gull Lake, everyone got along. Everyone was nice and helpful—wore a smile, gave lots of hugs and high-fives. Now I guess I'm back in the real world. People aren't all trying to be their best or look for ways to encourage you. They say mean things and do bad stuff. It's a bummer people can't be like the people at Gull Lake all the time."

The good news is that our life in eternity *will* be glorious, and there will be no sin or mean people. The bad news is that we live in a world that is full of sin. If we can try to spread some of God's joy down here, while we walk the earth, we can show what life *can* be. We can show love and joy right here and right now. It is all the more reason we need to be a blessing to others. There is a song that summarizes this sentiment very well, "Let There Be Peace on Earth, and Let It Begin with Me."

Have you ever been around people who you knew were withholding a blessing? Maybe there was the perfect opportunity for them to give a well-deserved compliment or acknowledgement and they decided not to do it. Maybe later they said they didn't want them to get a "big head" or thought they didn't truly deserve the accolades. Maybe there was some jealousy there. Sometimes they fear that they will be misunderstood and people will be thinking they were doing it to receive something in return. Maybe they were afraid they would be taken advantage of. If they do this now, it will be expected forevermore. For whatever reason, they withheld a blessing.

We have to remember that lighting someone else's candle doesn't make our candles less bright. It actually brightens the whole room. When we share our light, more people can shine for the Lord. It doesn't take anything away from us.

There are people who seem to have more money than they know what to do with, but when asked to give to a charity or donate toward a mission, they give very little or not at all. Yet you will see someone who has very little, who maybe even struggles to make ends meet, and that person gives *more* than expected. I've certainly witnessed both kinds of people. We don't know their whole stories, but they definitely make an impression on either side of the coin, don't they?

I encourage my students to always try to see the good in others and point it out to them. It doesn't cost anything to give a compliment. You never know when a simple compliment or a few words to show you care about them or notice they even exist, can make an impact. All people matter. God loves ALL of his people, and we are called to do the same. He died for all of us, not just those who go to church, obey the law, or read the Bible. We need to spread the word about this to those who don't know or maybe have forgotten. Jesus explicitly tells us this in Matthew 28:19–20, "Therefore, go and make disciples of all the nations, baptizing them in the name of the Father and the Son and the Holy Spirit. Teach these new disciples to obey all the commands I have given you. And be sure of this: I am with you always, even to the end of the age."

In the classroom, an activity I do the first month of school is to help kids recognize that everyone is special. They need to understand that no one is better than anyone else and that we were all given different abilities, talents, and gifts. When we can learn to recognize the differences in others, we can be more open minded and accepting.

We have one student each day that we showcase for the project. The students are asked to pay special attention to that person all day. At the end of the day, that student decorates a manila envelope, while the rest of the kids get a piece of paper to write down positive things they have noticed. It can be things they notice that day, from being in class with them during that month, or even outside of school. For example, if the student you are writing about is in your gymnastics class, you could give a compliment about that person's perseverance or ability to do various stunts.

The students are asked to write several things about the person. They cannot just write something like, "He is nice and fun." This is an activity that requires thoughtfulness. I truly want them to think about the receiver and how that person will feel when reading each page. I tell the kids to help that student feel special, noticed, and important.

After the students are finished writing their kind words, I collect the pages and place them in the manila envelope and keep it behind my desk. I also write something for every single student. (The kids usually look for my note first, so I try to make it long and impactful.) We do this for every student in the room and then have a reveal day. This is such a special day. I pass out all of the envelopes, and we count down from five to when we get to open them.

They tear open their envelopes with eagerness. They can't wait to see what their classmates think of them. Knowing that each student could only write positive things about them, it is a risk-free activity. Smiles abound, and some kids run over and give hugs to the writers of their notes. I've even had a few students cry happy tears. The power in this activity is that every person feels special and knows that everyone in the room sees something good. This can be an awesome reminder when times get tough or there is some drama between a couple students later in the year.

I've had students who did this years ago say that they still have their envelope and like to pull it out on a bad day. I know I have a file at school with happy notes and sweet letters from people that cheer me up when I am feeling discouraged. What if we could send notes like this occasionally for no reason at all, other than to uplift someone? Why don't we do this more often? We know it makes a difference.

There are kids who didn't realize something others recognized in them. Some may believe the bad things people tell them or don't believe they are worthy of goodness or love. They aren't used to being lifted up or praised for something. We need to be sure that it isn't just the winners and achievers who get all of the positive attention.

Our church live streams our services to a county jail. The pastor even goes to the jail to minister to them and has baptized many inmates. They are all invited to come to our church when they get out. I've witnessed some amazing testimonies from some of these people. For many, it is the first time they felt accepted and loved for good reasons. Some thought they'd blown their chances to be a Christian or didn't feel like they would be welcomed in a church.

When they understand the saving grace of God and that they can be forgiven no matter what they've done, it is life-changing. God loves these people just as he loves all sinners. We are called to love all of God's people, regardless of their sin nature because we are all sinners. You can find this in Romans 3:23–24, "For everyone has sinned; we all fall short of God's glorious standard. Yet God, in his grace, freely makes us right in his sight. He did this through Christ Jesus when he freed us from the penalty for our sins."

I know for me, my selfishness usually manifests itself in the use of my time. Our family seems to be very busy. Most of the time the things we are doing are good things. We are working to earn money, attending church, working on projects, coaching, studying, learning at conferences, getting groceries, running other errands, or taking care of life. This is not an excuse. I just think that if it doesn't make it on the calendar or to-do list, it doesn't happen. This is why I bought the Deed Diary and created an intentional plan to spread kindness and think of others more.

We needed some accountability to keep blessing others on our to-do list.

Prayer

> Lord, thank you so much for your grace when we don't give like we should. Please nudge us when we are self-focused and too busy to notice others' needs. Help us to remember to be good representatives of Christ and our family of believers. Help us to be generous in our actions and to serve with a happy heart.

Reflection

1. Can you think of a time you withheld a blessing? Maybe it was not giving a compliment or not offering to serve in some way that you could have? What caused you to pause and not act?

2. Why is it so important to represent our Christian identity outside of church? What do others gain or lose by this?

3. In 2 Corinthians 9:7 we are told, "For God loves a person who gives cheerfully." Why is it important to give with a happy heart?

4. What is one thing you can tell yourself the next time
   you think about saying "no" to an opportunity to bless
   someone?

CHAPTER 10

Why It's Worth It

We praise God for the glorious grace he has poured out on us who belong to his dear Son. He is so rich in kindness and grace that he purchased our freedom with the blood of his Son and forgave our sins. He has showered His kindness on us, along with all wisdom and understanding. God has now revealed to us His mysterious will regarding Christ- which is to fulfill His own good plan. And this is the plan: At the right time he will bring everything together under the authority of Christ- everything in heaven and on earth. Furthermore, because we are united with Christ, we have received an inheritance from God, for he chose us in advance, and he makes everything work out according to his plan. (Ephesians 1:6–11)

Again, we are not earning our spot in heaven with acts of kindness or by doing good, but we do have to account for our good and bad deeds. When we leave the earth, our first judgment from the great white throne will be to see if we are recorded in the Book of Life. If our name is not there, we do not enter heaven's gates. If we are in the Book of Life, 2 Corinthians 10:5 says, "We must all stand before Christ to be judged. We will each receive whatever we deserve for the good or evil we have done in this earthly body."

again

God wants us to show our faith while on this earth by bearing fruit. Our major purposes in life are to love God, glorify him, and love others. As we strive to live out our purposes, we are working on becoming holy, or sanctified. As we make progress toward holiness, Galatians 5:22– 23 says, "[T]he Holy Spirit produces this kind of fruit in our lives: love, joy, peace, patience, kindness, goodness, faithfulness, gentleness, and self-control." These are known as the fruit of the Spirit.

In John 15:8 Jesus says, "When you produce much fruit, you are my true disciples. This brings great glory to my Father." We can show and share our fruit through our acts of kindness and compassion. We can pray for God to put people in our paths that need our help. He will provide the opportunities to carry out his perfect plan.

What could be better than being considered one of Jesus's disciples and bringing God great glory? It is such a gift already that we were chosen by God. God loves us so much and by loving others, we can show our appreciation.

Did you know that most people believe what the most important person in their life believes about them? If you ever had a parent tell you something negative, you may believe that parent. If a good friend says something awful about you, you may think it's true. This is why you need to make Jesus the most important person in your life. Do you know what he believes about you? He says you are God's masterpiece; you are chosen; you are loved. You can believe what Jesus says about you.

Colossians 3:12 tells us, "Therefore as God's chosen people, holy and dearly loved, *clothe* yourselves with compassion, kindness, humility, gentleness, and patience" (italics mine). Pastor Rick Warren says that we should wake up and ask ourselves, "What kind of attitude am I going to wear today?" (God's Power to Change Your Life, p.119.) We can clothe ourselves spiritually as we set off to work for God's purposes.

When we try to lead a life that looks more like Jesus, we go through several stages. We have to accept Jesus as our Savior as Romans 6:7 says, "For when we died with Christ we were set free from the power of sin. This is the only way to the Father." We cannot go to heaven without this step. God saves us and makes us good, despite our sin nature. It is a gift that we can't earn and we don't deserve.

When we go through this stage, we are repenting of and setting aside our old ways through Christ's death on the cross. We are made new, which is why it is called being "reborn." You are given the power and desire to do good from God.

Once we are made new, Christ wants us to become more like him. We can do this by producing less and less sin and more and more fruit. There are many ways we can work toward bearing more fruit and becoming more obedient to his calling. Romans 6:16 says, "Don't you realize that you become the slave to whatever you choose to obey? You can be a slave to sin, which leads to death, or you can choose to obey God, which leads to righteous living." We want to be a slave to God rather than sin, of course. But it is easier said than done.

Here are some ways that Pastor Rick Warren suggests in *God's Power to Change Your Life* for learning to do good rather than sin: master your Bible, guard your mind, develop convictions, muster the courage to be different, and meet with other believers. (pp.146-153)

1. Master Your Bible – read it, use it, believe it, and study it.
2. Guard Your Mind – exercise self-control to avoid temptations to sin.
3. Develop Convictions – we are called to hate what is evil and cling to what is good.
4. Muster the Courage to Be Different – don't try to fit in when you were made to stand out. Shine a light for Jesus.

5. Meet with Other Believers – encourage one another to lead good lives.

If we continue to do these things and bear the fruit of the Spirit, our motives for obeying go from a fear of punishment to a desire to please him. Instead of thinking that we owe God, we want to do good out of a joy of his greatness and the beauty of his holiness. As we learn more about how to be better, we desire to do better. As you learn, you discern. We have to be our best in order to bless.

This process of becoming more like Jesus is not an easy path, but it is worth it, as the title of this chapter states. Satan will try really hard to get in the way of your blessings. He will temp you and distract you. You have to hold fast to Jesus and keep trying to be more like him. We will not be completely sanctified and sinless until we go to be with him. However, from the day we accept Jesus as our Savior, we are to be progressing toward becoming holy.

One of the biggest reasons it is worth it is because we have the opportunity to bring others into God's kingdom by shining a light for him and stirring the hearts of those around us. When we bring glory to God, people see him in us. They want to know why we have an inner joy, an inner peace, and kindness beyond understanding. People can become curious and yearn for him because they see this. How wonderful to share the *greatest* gift on earth?

Prayer

> Lord, thank you for calling us yours and for giving us the desire to bear the fruit of the Spirit and be more like you every day. I pray that Satan will stay out of our way, that we will continue to learn and grow our biblical knowledge, and that we will

have the courage to stand out instead of blend-
ing in. Please continue to guide us on our path to
sanctification. When we do good for others and
lead them to you, we know it is worth it.

Reflection

1. Which of the fruits of the Spirit are your strengths and
   which are more challenging for you (love, joy, peace, patience, kindness, goodness, and faithfulness)?

2. In what ways do you work on mastering your Bible?

3. How often do you meet with or fellowship with other
   believers?

4. Hebrews 10:10 says, "For God's will was for us to be made
   holy by the sacrifice of the body of Jesus Christ, once for
   all time." What steps have you taken to be more like him?

CHAPTER 11

A Challenge for Your Family

John 13:34–35: "So now I am giving you a new commandment: Love each other. Just as I have loved you, you should love each other. Your love for one another will prove to the world that you are my disciples."

Last Christmas, our family began a Bible study on the book *Don't Waste Your Life* by John Piper. We each had our own copy and read a chapter every week to discuss on Sunday evenings. This book opened our eyes to the much bigger picture of why and how we need to make our lives count.

What started years ago as a challenge to find opportunities to be kind turned into something much more significant. Doing a deed a day was a wonderful way to start seeking ways to serve, to learn the joy of giving, and to show God's love through our actions. What could be better than that outcome?

Over time, we realized our faith needed a boost, just as much as our selfish attitudes at the time. John Piper taught us that we shouldn't waste our lives. He said, "Desire that your life count for something great. Long for your life to have eternal significance." He further explained his belief, "Because I was created by God for His glory, I will magnify Him as I respond to His great love." (Don't Waste Your Life, 2003)

In the study, we asked ourselves things like:

How will my choices help me treasure Christ more?
How can I find ways to know Christ better?
How will my actions display Christ?

I love the analogy John Piper used in the book about TV commercials. He said that you could see an amazing commercial on TV that impresses you, but if the product isn't mentioned at all, what is the point?

This is a comparison to something impressive that we might do for others. What is the point if we don't mention who it's all about? We should behave and use God's creation in ways that draw attention to *him*. What we do should awaken worship. We should serve others in a way that gives God the glory and praise, not us.

Another book I've studied recently is Rick Warren's *Purpose Driven Life*. I have to admit, when I first bought the book over ten years ago, I read the first chapter and was so daunted by how far I was from living for Christ that I put it in a drawer. Pastor Rick's teachings are very convicting yet inspiring. I had to "warm" up to him by listening to his podcasts for several months before I was ready to try reading it again.

These two books, *Don't Waste Your Life* and *Purpose Driven Life*, are both heavy on the same message: God has an amazing plan and purpose for us while here on earth. As Ephesians 2:10 says, "For we are God's masterpiece. He has created us anew in Christ Jesus, so we can do the good things he planned for us long ago."

My family and I learned so much through our experiences recording a deed a day and intentionally reaching out to serve others. The Bible is full of Scripture that makes it *pretty* clear we are to be using our gifts to do this:

- Ephesians 4:7: "However, he has given each one of us a special gift through the generosity of Christ."

- First Corinthians 12:11: "It is the one and only Spirit who distributes all these gifts. He alone decides which gift each person should have."
- First Corinthians 12:7: "A spiritual gift is given to each of us so we can help each other."
- Mark 10:45: "For even the Son of Man came not to be served but to serve others and to give his life as a ransom for many."
- First Peter 4:10: "God has given each of you a gift from his great variety of spiritual gifts. Use them well to serve one another."
- Romans 12:8: "If your gift is to encourage others, be encouraging. If it is giving, give generously. If God has given you leadership ability, take the responsibility seriously. And if you have a gift for showing kindness to others, do it gladly."

Regarding gifts, John Piper says this, "The greatest joy in God comes from giving His gifts away, not is hoarding them for ourselves. It is good to work to have. It is better to work and have, in order to give." (Don't Waste Your Life, 2003)

Our other big understanding was how much we are loved by God and that we are called to love him. The word "love" is in the Bible over 645 times. God wants us to know that he loves us, wants us to love him, and wants us to show this love to others. When Jesus was asked the most important commandment in the law of Moses, he replied, "You must love the Lord your God with all your heart, all your soul, and all your mind. This is the first and greatest commandment. A second is equally important: Love your neighbor as yourself."(Matthew 22: 37-39)

Here are just a few passages that teach about how we are called to love:

- First John 3:18–19: "Dear children, let's not merely say that we love each other; let us show the truth by our actions. Our actions will show that we belong to the truth, so we will be confident when we stand before God."
- John 13:34–35: "A new commandment I give to you, that you love one another: just as I have loved you, you also are to love one another. By this all people will know that you are my disciples, if you have love for one another."
- First Corinthians 13:13: "Three things will last forever- faith, hope, and love- and the greatest of these is love."
- Galatians 5:14: "For the whole law can be summed up in this one command: "Love your neighbor as yourself."
- John 15:17: "This is my command: Love each other."
- Deuteronomy 6:5: "And you must love the Lord your God with all your heart, all your soul, and all your strength."

Just reading through 1 John 4, you can see how very much God loves us. How awesome is that? We can trust God's love because God IS love. Verses 17–19 proclaim such good news for us:

> And as we live in God, our love grows more perfect. So we will not be afraid on the day of judgment, but we can face him with confidence because we live like Jesus here in this world. Such love has no fear, because perfect love expels all fear. If we are afraid, it is for fear of punishment, and this shows that we have not fully experienced his perfect love. We love each other because he loved us first.

So, after reading this far, if you are convinced of God's love and the importance of sharing this love in his name, what are you waiting for? What can you do right now, today, to take a step toward intentionally blessing others in some way? How can you give out some secondhand blessings? What could your family do to spread his joy?

Sometimes when we know something is good to do, we still resist it because it can be hard to do, take too much time, or not feel like a priority. Think about exercising. We may drag our feet to get out the door to go to the gym or go for a walk, But when you return home after a good workout, don't you feel great? Don't you feel satisfaction in knowing you did something you were meant to do and that was good for you? I've often been reluctant to go for a run on a very hot or very cold day, but I've never regretted it after it was over!

You will never regret being kind to someone either. It may seem like a big effort or bother if you are really busy. But when you do take the time to do something meaningful for people, their smile will take away all of those feelings. You'll never think, "Man, I wish I hadn't made that person so happy," or "darn it, now they know God loves them."

We definitely need to get our heart in the right place to be cheerful givers. We need to be thoughtful. Just as I discouraged students from writing, "He's nice and he's fun," as their words of kindness, we need to be thoughtful in what we do for others. A Christmas gift of something you really like may be no gift at all to someone who doesn't enjoy the same things as you. For example, my daughter knows how to knit and would love to get new knitting supplies for a gift, but if she gave the same thing to me, it wouldn't be as precious. (I don't know how to knit and don't really want to learn how to do that particular skill.)

If you've ever heard of the book The Five Love Languages by Gary Chapman, you know that he shares the different ways in which people feel most loved and appreciated. It is an attempt to look at the receiver and plan something that will mean something to that person as an act of love. It was originally intended as a book for showing love to your mate, but the principles hold true for any relationships you have in your life.

Gary Chapman said the "love languages" are: words of affirmation, acts of service, receiving gifts, quality time, and physical touch. You may be able to think of someone who enjoys one or more of these gifts over another. Think about which of these means the most to you. When we are setting out to bless someone, we can try to keep these things in mind. If it is a total stranger, you wouldn't know which of these would be best, but in a given situation, it may become obvious.

For example, a busy mom wrangling a couple of small kids and a handful of groceries is probably going to appreciate a warm smile and having you get the door for her. A hungry homeless person may appreciate a hamburger more than anything else at a given moment. An elderly resident in a care facility may really cherish your time with a visit more than anything else. Someone you know who is suffering may need words of encouragement.

For people in your life whom you do know well, try to reach out in the love language that they would appreciate or need the most. This is not only being a blessing but also showing extra thoughtfulness as you meet their individual needs.

Taking the time to do something nice for someone you don't know well means a lot too. The next time you stay at a hotel, you could leave a special note and/or a small token of appreciation for the person cleaning your room. When someone waits on you at a restaurant or service desk, ask how the person is and really listen. Show that you care about that person. That person will remember that interaction. This is even more special if you do these intentional acts in front of your children. They need to see how you carefully plan or take time to care for others. They need to see you as a role model for kindness in a world where they are seeing all kinds of things modeled.

If you decide to do a deed a day with your family, there are many things to keep in mind. Doing this isn't to create a check-off list for kindness. It is so much more. It's important to share the why behind being kind. Kids need to also see the impact of kindness firsthand, from stories in the Bible to the direct results of their own acts of kindness. Most importantly though, kids need to understand that they are showing God's love through their actions. They are representatives of Christ and need to act as such.

One of the best parts of doing the Deed Diary for us was the dinner conversations that resulted. We sat down together for dinner each night and not only recorded our acts of kindness but also talked about the impacts we had. This is not to shine a light on us or pat ourselves on the back. It is to shine Christ's light *through* us and discuss the ripple effect this can have on someone's journey of faith or mental mindset.

When people are the recipients of a kind act, many things happen. They know they are thought of. They know they were deemed worthy of your time or resources. They may feel relief for having a need met. Hopefully, if you did it joyfully, they are inspired by your thoughtfulness and want to be kind to others in return. Hopefully they see your heart, and it could even start a conversation about who is in there.

Sometimes our acts of kindness are done privately. Maybe you prayed for people regularly during a tough time and they don't even know about it. Maybe you paid a bill for people and they never found out who did it. God will bless you for being his hands and feet and not seeking the treasures for it here below. When you have conversations at dinner about these kinds of gifts, your kids will understand the reason we do things. They need to know the power of prayer and who should get the praise for what we do.

So, my challenge for you is to get a notebook. Decorate it if you like, but it's not necessary. Have the family meeting. Share examples and Scriptures to be sure everyone understands. Then, just start. The first dozen days are important to get into the habit before it becomes more automatic. Depending on what you research, a habit can take three to five weeks to develop some automaticity. Don't stop. If you hit a rough patch, notice it and get back on track.

Just like with a diet, if you blow it on vacation one week, fess up, then get back on track, remembering why you started in the first place. I'm telling you, this experiment was life-changing for our family. We started it as an intentional way to think of others, but it grew our relationship as family members and grew our faith. What could be better than that?

Try it for a full year. Don't worry if you forget some days. Even when the year is up, this experience will stick with you and your kids. You will become more conscious of intentional kindness and won't want to withhold blessings. You'll see serving others as the opportunity to be God's hands and feet. You can't "un-feel" that just as you can't "un-know" that God calls us to love others.

The money we have, the talents we were born with, and the time we've been given are not ours. These are all from God. We have to be good stewards of God's resources.

I asked our oldest daughter, Emily, what she remembers most about doing a deed a day years ago. She said, "It made me go out of my way at least once a day to do something nice for another person because I knew that we would be sharing what we did together at dinner each night. I also enjoyed being able to hear what all of you did that day and how it affected others."

Our youngest daughter, Maddie, said, "It made me be more intentional about being considerate. As I went through my day, I was looking for opportunities to jump in and do something to help or to be nice."

My husband, Matt, said, "It was a way for me to notice good things happening and be a part of that through kindness. As a police officer, I see a lot of 'bad deeds' being done. I often see the worst in people. This helped me see the good in people."

This whole book is my reflection on the experience. I'm the most thankful for the impact it has had in growing our faith and the faith of others. As you embark on this experiment with your family, I hope it leads your heart to stretch past your comfort zone sometimes. I hope it gives you a yearning to know God more intimately. Maybe your family can do some book or Bible studies together. Encourage each other as you do this important work. May God bless you richly.

Prayer

> Lord, thank you for the person reading this book. I pray that you would bless this person for taking the time to learn more about being your hands and feet. As we strive to be more like you, I pray for wisdom when we feel stuck, courage when we feel uncomfortable, and compassion when we seek out those in need. We love you and look forward to the day that we meet you and hear you say, "Well done, my good and faithful servant."

Reflection

1. How do you teach compassion to your children? In what ways have you seen them exhibit compassion? In what ways could they expand on this?

2. Read Psalm 145: "Your awe-inspiring deeds will be on every tongue: I will proclaim your greatness. Everyone will share the story of your wonderful goodness; they will sing with joy about your righteousness." How can we use this

stirring in our hearts to do good and share why we desire to do this?

3. What are some ways your family could serve together? What examples can you give that you have already done?

4. John C. Maxwell says, "When I die, I cannot take with me what I have, but I can live in others by what I gave." (Intentional Living, p. 24, 2015) What does he mean by this?

One Hundred Ideas to Get You Started

1. Hold the door for someone.
2. Give someone a compliment.
3. Pray for someone.
4. Do your chores without being asked.
5. Do someone else's chore without being asked.
6. Pick up trash.
7. Donate towels, blankets, or toys to the animal shelter.
8. Donate food to the food pantry.
9. Drop off treats to the police or fire station.
10. Send a thank-you note to someone.
11. Hide a dollar in the dollar store for someone to find.
12. Pay for the car behind you in the drive-thru.
13. Tape change to a pop machine.
14. Leave microwave popcorn on the Redbox machine.
15. Visit people in a care center.
16. Give a welcome note and small treat to a new student.
17. Leave a positive note in library books or a new book mark.
18. Use sidewalk chalk to write positive messages in parks and school entrances.
19. Give someone a "heart attack" by posting a bunch of heart-shaped messages on the desk or door.
20. Write a positive review for a book you enjoy.
21. Donate to your favorite cause.
22. Invite a friend to go for a walk or a bike ride.
23. Find an old picture of a friend or family member and send it with a note about the special memory.
24. Give your pastor a card of appreciation for something specific.
25. Serve others as a family. (Ring salvation army bell, go on a mission trip, or serve in a soup kitchen.)
26. Rake someone's leaves.
27. Shovel someone's drive or sidewalk.

28. Wash someone's car.
29. Take someone out to lunch or make lunch for that person.
30. Rub your parents' shoulders.
31. Babysit for someone, free of charge.
32. Hand out flowers to random people and wish them a good day.
33. Send a birthday box to a shelter, with cake mix, frosting, and banners.
34. Share an encouraging verse with someone.
35. Post a message on social media about how great you think someone in your community is.
36. Give your favorite book to someone.
37. Give love coupons for favors that can be redeemed at any time.
38. Leave someone a nice message taped up in the house where that person will find it.
39. Give out freshly baked cookies to neighbors or friends.
40. Make a double batch of whatever you're having for dinner and drop off the extra to a busy mom.
41. Get tickets to an event on a night you know the person doesn't have plans to surprise that person.
42. Donate toys and diapers to the nursery of a church.
43. Donate feminine items and makeup to a crisis center for abused women.
44. Clean for someone who is ill or going through a tough time.
45. Play music or sing at a care center or church.
46. Invite someone out for coffee.
47. Give someone a house-warming gift.
48. Leave coupons by the items in the store they can be redeemed for.
49. Instead of having a garage sale, donate your items.
50. Pray for family, friends, and coworkers.
51. Offer someone going to the same place a ride.
52. Walk someone's dog.

53. Send encouraging texts on the dates of tough events or appointments.
54. Leave a sweet note in your spouse's car.
55. Set the table or clear the table.
56. Run an errand for someone.
57. Go above and beyond for your next carry-in lunch.
58. Send a care package to a soldier.
59. Send finals treats to a student in college.
60. Bring soup and a box of tissues to someone who is sick.
61. Give a bigger tip than usual around the holidays.
62. Buy from the girl scouts, boy scouts, and kids in various clubs doing fundraisers.
63. Volunteer in a classroom.
64. Support a missionary or send a letter of encouragement.
65. Take your shopping cart back in the store when you are finished with it.
66. Cut out pictures of people you know in the newspaper and send the clippings with a congratulatory message.
67. Sit by someone sitting alone at lunch.
68. Help carry groceries into the house.
69. Hide a note in a family member's suitcase.
70. Invite someone to go to church with you.
71. Let someone go ahead of you in line.
72. Post favorite Bible verses around the house or at work.
73. Give your seat up for someone on the bus.
74. Smile and say hello to strangers.
75. Donate new coloring books and crayons to children's hospitals.
76. Pay a toll for someone behind you.
77. Donate blood.
78. Leave a treat in your mailbox for the mail carrier.
79. Leave a blessing bag in your car for a homeless person.
80. Leave detergent and/or dryer sheets at the laundromat.

81. Send a note to a teacher or coach about how that person has made a difference.
82. Try to make it a whole day with no negative comments.
83. Tell a boss or manager about a job well done by one of the employees.
84. Invite someone to a holiday meal who has no one to spend the holidays with.
85. Sponsor a child.
86. Offer to host a New Year's Eve party for kids so their parents can go out.
87. Tape up positive messages on mirrors in public bathrooms.
88. Pay someone's library fine.
89. Take a group of kids Christmas caroling.
90. Give blood.
91. Be an organ donor.
92. Knit hats and scarves for a school to give out to kids who need them.
93. Take someone to a movie or play.
94. Give someone a long hug who needs it.
95. Send someone a picture of a fond memory with that person.
96. Give your time to someone who needs it.
97. Run or walk a 5K for a good cause.
98. Ask for donations to a charity for your birthday.
99. Make muffins or cookies and bring them to work to share.
100. Mentor someone younger than you.

About the Author

Shannon Anderson is a teacher, speaker, author, and child of God trying do her best to serve others and be God's hands and feet. She was born and raised in Indiana, where she shares her home with her police-hero hubby, Matt, and two daughters, Emily and Maddie. She prays that through her faith journey, her children and those around her may see her heart and who is in there.